Weber offers a much-needed, open, and honest resource for a type of loss culturally we push under the rug. In offering her story and recognizing the many, many dynamics that reveal themselves when a child is lost, Weber begins an important conversation. This book will be helpful if you've experienced your own loss, or for the individual or congregation that wants to respond better to the mothers, fathers, sisters, and brothers all around us who mourn, while still rejoice, with their child, in the arms of Christ.

—Deaconess Heidi Goehmann, writer, blogger,
and speaker at I Love My Shepherd Ministries

Never Forsaken

GOD'S MERCY IN THE MIDST OF MISCARRIAGE

KATHRYN ZIEGLER WEBER

CONCORDIA PUBLISHING HOUSE • SAINT LOUIS

Published by Concordia Publishing House
3558 S. Jefferson Ave., St. Louis, MO 63118-3968
1-800-325-3040 • www.cph.org

Manufactured in the United States of America

Library of Congress Cataloging-in-Publication Data

Names: Weber, Kathryn Ziegler, author.
Title: Never forsaken : God's mercy in the midst of miscarriage / Kathryn Ziegler Weber.
Description: Saint Louis : Concordia Publishing House, [2018] | Includes bibliographical references.
Identifiers: LCCN 2018018906 (print) | LCCN 2018027867 (ebook) | ISBN 9780758660114 | ISBN 9780758660053
Subjects: LCSH: Consolation. | Mothers--Religious life. | Miscarriage--Religious aspects--Christianity.
Classification: LCC BV4907 (ebook) | LCC BV4907 .W38 2018 (print) | DDC 248.8/66--dc23
LC record available at https://lccn.loc.gov/2018018906

1 2 3 4 5 6 7 8 9 10   27 26 25 24 23 22 21 20 19 18

ACKNOWLEDGMENTS

I would like to thank, first and foremost, my husband and daughter for their patience with me as I fumbled through my obligations as wife, first-time mom, and author. I would also like to thank and acknowledge all the women for whom this book is intended. I am indebted to each of the contributing mothers who brought the studies to life by sharing their personal and sometimes raw stories of loss: Kristina Odom, Melissa A. DeGroot, Rebecca Kearney, Kendra Voss, Kristen Gregory, Audrey Daenzer, Melissa Jones, and Stephanie Traphagan. Without them, this book would lack depth, application, and diversity. Thanks is also owed to those who helped me gather information from abroad, including Rosie Adle, Kristina Rutledge Phillips, Daniel Fickenscher, the Rev. Hans Fiene, and the Rev. Mark Surburg. Much appreciation is also due to Concordia Publishing House for making this book a possibility and to all whose hands have helped bring this book to print.

TABLE OF CONTENTS

ADDITIONAL RESOURCES:

PREFACE

I believe in the Holy Spirit, the holy Christian church, the communion of saints, the forgiveness of sins, the resurrection of the body, and the life everlasting, Amen. (Third Article of the Apostles' Creed)

When I speak the words "resurrection of the body," I cross myself in remembrance of my Baptism. This isn't something I was taught as a child, but rather something that became important to me as I grew in my faith. Why? Why is this simple gesture (though perhaps a little too pious for some) important to me? It is something I do to show "This is what I believe." It is a tangible action that connects me to the very real water and Word poured over me when I was too young to understand. Then, when I found out I was pregnant, I would discreetly place my hand upon my tummy before crossing myself and make a tiny sign of the cross with my thumb where I imagined my baby to be. This was not only a comfort in the moment; it would become a greater solace for me later.

So in weakness and in health, I cross myself, and most times I look forward to saying those comforting words of the Creed—"the resurrection of the body." *Most* times I look forward to saying them. In my weakness, my confession in word and action may be less than convincing. Yet even at my weakest, the words, the promise, and the movement are the anchor to which I cling.

I had experienced death before I ever miscarried, and I learned at a young age that death, loss, and grief are constant visitors this side of eternity. When loved ones died, I went through a period of mourning and grieving. I learned to remember them with fondness and hope for a blessed reunion in heaven. There is something unique, however, about the loss of life within your own body. And although the circumstances are different for everyone experiencing infant loss, the grief is very profound and creates the same needs.

With the children who have died in my womb, I have learned that the only hope I have to cling to is Christ. There are no souvenirs of their existence or memories to hold onto, not even a promise of meeting them as healthy newborns cradled in the arms of my Savor. There are only the promises of Christ alone. So, I cling to His resurrection and the promise of wholeness therein.

The only meaning and justification I can find for having to move through grief is that it produces a greater dependence upon Christ. Among the many recurring themes of miscarriage and infant loss, there are two that presently stick out in my mind:

- finding meaning for the pain and loss—the "Why?"; and
- finding peace or resolution—the "How?"

These two questions often create a vicious cycle of thought: *If I could just know why it happened, then I would know how to move forward.* Often, though, answers to these questions aren't good enough. The "why" of pain and "how" to escape it are not found within ourselves or in the little shrines we build and rituals we create to try to give deeper meaning to our suffering. In fact, there is no explanation for it. There is only a remedy—Christ. But that truth can be less than satisfying because of our sinful ways of understanding and grieving.

With my miscarriage came many false hopes for getting better and finding healing within. I had created a dark room inside my head, and my heart found it comfortable and comforting to dwell there. That room is grief. It is always there. It is an impenetrable room where I convinced myself that only I was allowed to enter. In that room, I didn't know what to do with myself; sometimes I didn't know how to get out of it. Some days I didn't *want* to get out. It was comfortable to just sit and do nothing. Grief has a way of not just being a visitor but a constant companion, and it takes time to learn to live with it. It took time for me to realize that I would never find my lost children in that room. I couldn't even remember them well, no matter how long I sat and reflected. In that room, I held only the gory details of their lives: the pain, the suffering, the helpless waiting to learn whether this child would live to take his or her first breath, the silent ultrasounds. It took time for me to discover that the only way I would be able to appropriately remember them was to find another way.

Grief forces us to grow up in ways we would never invite and could never imagine. The stages of grief become things we work through daily and move through, like a ritual or a creed, a cycle we work through but never quite move out of. Grieving is something for us to do even as we long for and miss the lives we had hoped to carry into this world, nurture, care for, and send off into the world on their own.

I realized that I needed to leave my darkened room and walk down a road as a pilgrim setting off on a journey of reflection and discovery. The road may have twists, turns, and a darkened path, but it is a way forward nonetheless. Grief is not a place to sit alone; it is a journey on which we join others. Each of us deals with grief a little differently, and our experiences are unique—but the journey itself is not unique. One need look no further than the cross to realize that there is no escaping the pain and suffering that sin brought into this world. Christ walked the road to Calvary, a road well laid out by foreigners, thieves, sojourners, bloodthirsty murderers, and self-righteous law-abiders. His pilgrimage was not for Himself, because He wasn't anything but sinless and holy. No, His path to death was not for Himself; rather, He took that journey in order to be with the very people He came to die for and save. He took that road for us.

As we wait for the healing of our lowly bodies and the restoration in heaven of what was lost on earth, we cling to what we know. We continue to lift our weak arms and make the sign of the cross over our fragile bodies, knowing that God's power is made perfect in weakness. With feeble voices, we continue to recite the promises we have in the Creed. And with tear-filled eyes, we search the Word of God for our comfort. We believe in the resurrection of the body and the life everlasting. And if that is all that we can cling to in this time, then it is enough to know that we are never forsaken.

While feelings can deceive us in the midst of grieving, we are never forsaken in the midst of our suffering and loss. God's Word provides us with comfort and assurance that He is surely with us, even while we pass through the fires of life. We confess a God who has power over death, and we hold dearly to all those promises He offers us—especially His promise of presence.

I am delighted that you have decided to use this book on your own journey with grief. My heart breaks for the same reasons you have been moved to read it. My prayer for you is that God would use my journey and His Word to help guide you to see and better know your Savior in the midst of your suffering. Perhaps not all of these chapters will directly relate to you, but I hope that each will reveal something new and helpful for you in your pilgrimage with grief. I understand that the weight of the Law already hangs heavy upon the mother who has lost a child, but some of these chapters might challenge the baptized grieving mother to face ugly aspects of her grief in which sin can rear its nasty head. I pray that God would show you the good that only He can make of what may be some of your saddest days.

For now, know that you are not alone. The women who share the stories in these pages are faithful women who have braved the storms of miscarriage and infant loss and have come out on the other side. They still carry grief as a constant companion, but they also hold the joy of Christ in their hearts as they treasure up and ponder all the beautiful memories they had with their children while in the womb and, for some, while in the world.

May God bless you and keep you in the study of His Word and the contemplation of the life that He has given and that He has allowed to be taken away.

CHAPTER 1

WHY?

In this life, we are left with little explanation as to why some things happen. This study will address the peace God offers us through His Son amidst the frustration of so many unanswered questions. We will try to focus on Christ as the answer to all our "whys" even when we are left without answers.

VERSE FOR MEDITATION

For God alone my soul waits in silence; from Him comes my salvation.

Psalm 62:1

INTRODUCTION

Why? This question seems like a good place to start. Several years ago, I lived in the mission field with a family. Their oldest child at the time was four years old. She would delight in her bad influence over her two-year-old brother by teaching him words like "No!" and "Why?" Everything for the two of them became a protest or a question that demanded answers, and no matter the answer given, it was always followed with another "Why?" If you have experience with little children, then you know exactly how this never-ending process goes. If you are struggling with a miscarriage or infant loss, you also know how the vicious cycle of unanswered questions revolves in your head. You can be given all the technical answers, and you still ask, "Why? Why my child? Why me? Why my family?" Even if by some supernatural occurrence God came into your home to sit and sip tea, and He did answer these questions fully and completely, I believe His answer still would not be enough. What we really want is not answers but our children.

The following is a reflection from Kristina Odom. Kristina came to the United States from Finland to study theology. She met her husband at the seminary where they both studied together. They were later married and together they have grown a family. What she learned from her theological studies helped her as she faced the death of her second child. She reflects on what it means to ask questions in the midst of grief due to a miscarriage and due to infant loss.

How Long, O Lord?

It was a time of big changes in my little family's life. My husband had just finished his studies at the seminary, and we were preparing to move to his first call. Our daughter Edith was six months old, and before we made the big move, we traveled overseas to visit my family so they could meet her for the first time. Soon after the trip, we found out that I was pregnant again.

We moved and settled down and finally had our first doctor's appointment at fifteen weeks. The ultrasound showed that we were having another girl, but it also showed that there were some serious concerns. What followed was a whirlwind of doctors' appointments and then sad news. In week eighteen, we were given a diagnosis. Our baby girl had Down syndrome, but even more serious, a very severe heart defect. She had less than a 30 percent chance of surviving until week twenty-six, the time for our appointment with the pediatric cardiologist. Her heart was enlarged and would continue to grow and eventually begin to fail; this could also put my life in danger, as there was a risk for a "mirror syndrome" in which my heart could mimic her heart failure.

But our little Matilda Grace surprised everyone, and at that appointment she was doing wonderfully. She continued to do so until week thirty-six, despite her very enlarged heart. During these weeks of waiting and watching, we felt much anxiety and fear, but we were not asking very many "whys" yet. Those would come later. We prayed for healing, for the opportunity to meet her outside the womb while she was alive, and for faith so we would be able to say with Job, "The Lord gave, and the Lord has taken away; blessed be the name of the Lord" (1:21), even when He took our baby girl home to Himself.

The Lord answered some of our prayers with a yes. The day arrived when we would finally meet her. Matilda had not died in the womb; we would meet her while she was alive. Her heart was now failing, but she was still fighting!

Matilda was born via C-section on a beautiful winter morning. Much to everybody's surprise—again—she was well enough to cry. We heard her weak little cry and cried ourselves. And yet again, God answered our prayers with a yes. She was baptized and granted everlasting healing right there in the operating room. What a comfort this would be for us in the days, months, and years ahead. She was quickly brought to the NICU at the large children's hospital next door. For me, the day went by in post-op while the doctors and nurses tried to keep Matilda stable. Then, midafternoon, she suddenly crashed, and the nurses in the labor and delivery unit rushed me over to the NICU so I could see her. That trip seemed like a long wait while I pleaded with God to not take her yet. I had not yet seen her or held her; I had only briefly touched her hand before she was moved to the NICU. Once again, He answered my prayers with a yes. I saw and touched my beautiful daughter several times that afternoon and evening.

The next day Matilda had major heart surgery. The surgery was supposed to take six to eight hours but lasted eleven. The anxiety I felt was almost unbearable, and it only increased as the hours went by slowly. Again and again, I cried and pleaded with God that He would let me hold her before He took her home.

She spent the night in PICU in very critical condition. The next morning, we were called over by her doctors. The news was not good. She had had a massive brain hemorrhage during the surgery. There was nothing else to be done for her. Her heart was too weak to function without machines, and her brain had shut down. We spent the day with her, waiting for my parents and our other daughter to arrive. Edith visited her sister for the only time. Once everyone else had arrived, we took turns holding her. Then all life support was discontinued. I held her in my arms while she took her last breath here on earth.

God had answered our prayers. Yes, we did get to hold her before she died. No, He did not heal her here on earth but took her home to heaven.

The days, weeks, and months that followed are a blur. There are a few clear memories here and there, but mostly they are foggy. Leaving the hospital without my baby was heartbreaking. And that feeling persisted as I spent the next days going to the funeral home to finalize the arrangements, seeing her before and during the visitation, watching her casket as it was carried into and out of the church by my father and her godfather, then seeing it lowered into the ground. The aching, empty arms. The pain so overwhelming that it was hard to breathe. *My baby's body is in a dark hole in the ground!* The tears and the questions to God finally came. My husband was there to listen, hold me, and wipe my tears. But there were no answers.

With the questions came anger, kindled by the fact that my milk for my sweet baby came in the night she died. *Why don't you answer me, my dear husband? My God? Why did You take her? Why did she have to be so sick?*

We had said our good-byes, left her in the PICU, and gone back to labor and delivery for one last night. And there it felt like my body had betrayed me. I had been pumping and pumping for my baby with no result, but now that she didn't need it anymore, my breasts were full of milk.

Why, oh why, God? Why do You have to be so cruel? If You are almighty, could You not have prevented this from happening?

Matilda's death was the ultimate blow, and I could not stop dwelling on it, questioning God about it, and being angry with Him because of it. I knew the theologically correct answers to many of my questions: it is because of sin that she was so sick; Jesus has died and risen for her sickness and for all suffering; in Him we are all perfectly healed already, although not necessarily while we are here on earth; and so on. But that knowledge did not help me in my suffering when the unbearable pain made it difficult to breathe, when I didn't know how to survive the day. That knowledge only increased my anger.

Somehow the days and months went by. We lived through the pain every day, and we survived. I still don't know how. Our sweet Edith gave us a reason to get up in the morning and brought joy even to the darkest of days. Eleven months later I was pregnant again. We were so excited, only to meet more grief. The baby died at six weeks. On the one-year anniversary of Matilda's funeral, we lost baby Jesse.

We were back in the darkness, but this time we stayed busy with a new house and renovations. One month later I was pregnant again. This time I dared not hope. And sure enough, baby Jamie died at eight weeks.

We had lost three babies in fifteen short months. The pit was deeper and darker than ever, and the questions to God continued. Why, oh why do we have to lose not one, not two, but three babies? It's not fair. So many people have lots of children and never lose any. Why do we have to lose three? *Why do You do this to us?*

Why are You not answering?

Anger was my dominant emotion for a long time. Even simple comments such as "Praying for comfort and peace" made me angry because I felt that there was no room for peace. The pain was overwhelming. I felt like Rachel, refusing to be comforted because my children were no more (see Jeremiah 31:15; Matthew 2:18).

I could not see or feel it at the time, but just as the Lord promised to restore Israel in Jeremiah 31, He would restore me and bring me comfort in His good time. As the months went by, my anger subsided a little when

I realized that peace is not a feeling; it is a state of being. We have peace with God because of what Christ has done for us. Even if I don't feel at peace, my relationship to God is not changed. I am His child because Christ's merits were given to me in my Baptism. No suffering or pain can take that away, regardless of how I feel.

Not only did I question God, but I also had much doubt. I didn't doubt His existence, but I did, very strongly, doubt His love toward me. (How could He love me if He sent me so much suffering?) I doubted my own faith. (What did I even believe anymore, when I was so angry and questioned Him so much?) My husband assured me that my cries and "whys" to God were signs of faith: if I didn't believe in Him, I wouldn't go to Him with my questions.

Slowly the darkness lessened. God did not give my unending questions direct and specific answers, but He continued to speak through the Word that my pastor husband preached. I didn't want to hear it; the words about His love and mercy were too painful. How can He be loving and merciful yet bring me so much pain? Does He not care that I'm in agony?

Church was the worst and hardest place to be. I cried through so many sermons and services. I could not sing or pray; I could not even utter the words of the Lord's Prayer.

But church was also the most restful place to be. I heard. I received. Even if those words brought me more pain, they did not put more burdens on me. I did not have to be stoic and pretend to be doing well. My church family sat with me in my grief and accepted me where I was. I did not have to try to glorify God in my losses. I was allowed to cry and lament to Him and bring Him all my questions. I didn't even have to pray because my loved ones prayed for me when I couldn't. Even there I was on the receiving end, just as I am in the Divine Service where He gives me His Word and His Supper. As with everything in my relationship with my Lord, I don't have to—and I can't—do anything. All I do is receive His grace and rest in that.

I began to hear God's answers again. And what I heard was that it is His love and His mercy that have given me this burden to bear. It is a severe mercy but a mercy nonetheless. He loves me and is teaching me how much He loves me, what He has done for me, and what I am in myself. Through the heavy burden of grief, I learn that I'm not strong, that I can't get through this by myself. His main purpose for this is not that I would become a better person or better mother or better Christian. That is not why He gave me this to bear.

I learn that trust in Him, as the First Commandment teaches, doesn't come naturally to me. No matter how hard I try, I can't learn to trust Him more, not for my salvation, and also not in His wisdom and love for me when He leads me through dark valleys. Because of sin, I don't trust God completely and perfectly as the Law demands. All I can do is to repent.

It is certainly true that He also works sanctification through my suffering so that I do become more thankful for the gifts He gives me, such as my daughter Edith. I also see how my sinful nature always shows its ugly face in all things. The good works I do in my vocations—and maybe even become better at—are just that: good works for my neighbors.

But the Lord primarily uses my suffering to show me how dependent I am on Him for my salvation and for everything else. I'm too weak, helpless, sinful, and angry with God. If I'm honest, I have to admit that I want nothing to do with Him. I have to confess that if I am to make it home to heaven to see Jesus and see my babies again, I have nothing to do with it. During my darkest days, hearing that I should lean on Jesus offers me no comfort. These words are not the Gospel; they're the Law, so I have another burden to bear when I hear that I have to do something. Because of my sinful nature, I can't lean on Him, hold on to Him, believe or trust in Him. He has to hold on to me. And He does. He doesn't let me go. In His mercy, He feeds me with His Word and His Supper even when I don't want it. And little by little, His Means of Grace give new life to my soul.

I have tasted God's love. I would like to tell you that it is always a rich, delicious feast. But often, when watching my children suffer, I have to be satisfied with a tincture, just a taste. For the time being.

"Like a patient just waking up from surgery, I feel groggy. Pain. Hunger, yes. Some nausea. I am thirsty but leery of drinking too deep too fast. In and out, I am uncertain. At this point in my life, I cannot jump up and leap for joy. The sites of the Surgeon's amputations still throb. He will have to watch my wounds for infection, I think, very closely indeed."[1]

There were, however, two questions I never asked God during those most painful months and years. I did not ask, "Where are You, God? Why have You abandoned me?" I wanted to accuse Him of that too, but I knew the answer. I had studied the doctrine of vocation. I knew that He was hiding behind those around me. He was caring for me, wiping my tears, and listening to my questions through my dear husband. He was loving me and giving me a reason to live through my sweet daughter. He was reminding me that I was not forgotten through my sister, who, from the other side of the big ocean, sent me a message almost every day for many months. He was in church with me and holding my hand while I was crying during sermons through the kind old lady and dear friend sitting next to me. He was feeding me through my friends who made freezer meals for me after we lost Jamie.

He was close by. I saw Him everywhere, and as painful as it was, it was also the only thing that brought me some comfort. In my darkest days, not even the Gospel brought me comfort, but this knowledge did, at least a little. So I finally learned that when we in our suffering cry, "Where are You, God?" we lift our eyes too high and look too far. He is very close, coming to us, caring for us, and loving us through those He has put in our lives. And He comes even closer in the Divine Service, where He gives us forgiveness, life, and salvation through our pastors when we receive His Son's body and blood in our mouths.

Did this knowledge take away my pain and my questions? It didn't seem

---

1   Schultz, *The Problem of Suffering*, 54.

to immediately, but God used time to lessen my pain, calm my fears, quiet my questions, and strengthen my faith in Him. Almost five years after we lost Matilda, the overwhelming pain is gone; only sadness and longing remain, and I no longer need to have all my "whys" answered. Jesus' death and resurrection and my participation in that in my Baptism are enough. I know my babies are safely home, and I plead and beg that the Lord would keep me, my husband, and our other children in faith so we can join them one day.

Grief veils our vision. We don't always see things as clearly as we might have before. As Kristina so eloquently put it in her reflection, she knew God was present and that He was "hiding behind" those around her. When we are bombarded with so many questions, doubts, and concerns in the midst of grief, we can't always see that God is present, working, hearing our prayers, and answering the question of why He has become hidden to us. Yet He is constantly answering us through His Word, His presence in the Divine Service, and His people.

Grief can also make us forget or become deaf to what we have heard. We may already know the answers, but if you are like me, you will say several times throughout your journey, "Tell me again. I need to hear it again. Tell it to me a different way than before, even though you have already told me a thousand times. My head knows, but my heart needs to hear it again."

Throughout this book, we will look to God's Word and read it again and again to be reminded why God has allowed us to suffer and how He answers us and remains present, merciful, faithful, and compassionate to us in the midst of it all.

A Simple Understanding of "Why?"

1. **Our suffering is because of sin—not our sin specifically, just sin in general.** We are not immune to the effects of sin. It should not catch us off guard that we suffer in this life—yet it always does, and it always will. No matter how carefully we guard our lives, sin and death are always a present reality. And while we mourn the effects of sin and death, we also thank God for the joys that remain unscathed in our lives and for His faithfulness to us.

2. **We have Christ.** Christ is the atonement for our sin. When we suffer the effects of sin, we can look to the cross and know that there is the answer to all our questions. When we ask, "Why my baby?" God says, "Here, have My Son." God made our sufferings temporary and gave us His Son so that we may live in joy in the last.

3. **We trust in God's presence.** We can know God is present even in the silence of unanswered questions. While the silence may seem deafening at times, God promises us in His Word to be near the brokenhearted (Psalm 34:18). We can know that He is present with us in His Word and Sacraments and near us through the compassion of our neighbors.

Scripture Discussion and Reflection

The shock of death in the womb makes us acutely aware that our bodies are broken due to sin. The life and death that pass leave a mother not only with an awareness of her broken body and broken heart but with a plethora of unanswerable questions as well. "What was going on inside my womb for the time that I carried my baby?" "Was it caused by something I did or didn't do?" Questions can torment a grieving and broken heart. And unanswered questions can produce guilt, doubt, and anger.

This is why it becomes so important for a Christian to know and understand that it is due to the fall into sin that we are left with broken bodies that sometimes surprise us by failing and falling apart. Our broken bodies, however, have another message to proclaim apart from "pitiful broken-down sinner." Our broken bodies can remind us that restoration is coming, healing is coming, and wholeness is ours in Christ.

Open your Bible and read 1 Corinthians 15:51–58.

1. In verse 54, Paul writes, "When the perishable puts on the imperishable," which indicates that there is a specific time that this happens. When is that time?

2. How does holding on to the hope of resurrection and victory that we have in our Lord Jesus Christ offer answers to our "why" questions?

One of the best examples in the Bible of unjust treatment and questioning is that of Job. Job is a natural biblical connection for when we suffer and ask, "Why?" However, reading the Book of Job for comfort is futile, as it is not written to comfort but to show how faith responds in the midst of trial. Job loses it all; then he is poorly comforted by family and friends, is told to forsake God and die beside his wife. Yet we do, somehow, find comfort in seeing him suffer so much, wrestle with God, and still be able to make the great confession we read at the end of the book. Job's confession is an important anchor for all to cling

to in the midst of uncertainty and of asking, "Why?"
Read Job 19:23–26.

3. What are some of the significant points in Job's confession?

4. Why would Christ be a comfort and an answer for Job's "why" questions when considering the loss of his children, land, animals, and physical well-being?

Job's confession and hope were sure and certain for him. After all the trials he had been through and after doubting himself and questioning God, he clings to the confession he gives in verses 25–26.

We see a similar proclamation in Revelation 21:3–5. Read it now.

5. At what point in our life, in the whole of the Bible, and in this passage in particular do we see God "dwelling" with man?

6. What are the promises in Revelation that our sinful flesh can cling to when facing the death of our children?

One of the most powerful stories in the Bible is that of the death of Lazarus. It shows us Christ most clearly as fully man, sharing in our earthly struggles, and fully God, bringing the dead back to life.
Read John 11:1–44.

7. In verse 21, we see Martha making her own confession of who and what she knows Christ to be and to be capable of. Taking into consideration the text from Revelation 21:3–5, what does Martha confess but fail to realize?

8. This pericope (specific reading for a day of the Church Year) shows us how death causes confusion and causes us to ask many questions. What is one of the questions asked in our text, and what is significant in Christ's response? (Look at vv. 37, 40–42.)

9. According to the text, why did Christ allow Lazarus to die?

10. What caused Christ to weep, and why?

God Himself knows the never-ending interrogation that death

brings to its survivors. He knows full well that the wages of sin is death, and for that, He paid the price for us. While we sit in sackcloth, mourn, continually ask, "Why?" and challenge the many "what ifs" of our loss, Jesus responds in the same way He did when calling Lazarus from the tomb. He says to death itself: "Unbind him, and let him go" (John 11:44). He proclaims victory over death's power by commanding it to release us and let us go as well. As true God, Jesus has all authority in heaven and on earth, and He has the present power to fix all our earthly problems. Yet He waits, just as He did with Lazarus. He waits so we might know Him better, so we might learn to cling to His death and resurrection, His promises, and His healing. He gives us only one answer in the midst of questioning and grieving for our little ones, and that is Himself. The answer is Christ Jesus because it is He who has overcome sin, death, and the devil for us. It is Christ who freely offers us the same incorruptible flesh, put on us in the waters of Holy Baptism. Christ is the only answer because in this time, Christ is who we need most.

Personal Reflection

1. What are some of the questions to which you desperately feel that you want answers in the midst of your loss?

2. How do you think having your questions fully answered would help you in your grieving?

3. Do the three points of study listed earlier ("A Simple Understanding of 'Why?'") address your questions, and if so, how?

Homework

Take some time to write out all the questions that came to mind in the midst of your suffering. Formulate each question in terms of struggle, then turn it into a prayer that acknowledges God as the answer and peace for each doubt and question. For each question, address God, write out your struggle, write what you seek from Him (e.g., peace, pardon, comfort, and so on), and last, commend it to Christ.

Example

Address God: Heavenly Father,

Your struggle: I struggle daily with understanding what was medically wrong with my baby that (he or she) died before I could hold (him or her) and bring (him or her) to the waters of Holy Baptism.

What you seek: I trust that You know all things and that You are a merciful God, as You show us in Your Word. I entrust my cares and concerns to You in this time of grief. Give me peace and help me to always remember Your Son when I think about my own child, whom I long to hold in my arms and love.

Commend it to Christ: Through Jesus Christ, Your Son, our Lord. Amen.

PRAYER

Gracious heavenly Father, You know all things and have answered all our doubts and questions of "Why?" by giving Your one and only Son to know our life of struggle and pain and to ultimately die for us in order to bring us back to You. When questions of "Why?" taunt us, help us to focus on the cross and the promise we hold that is the same for us as it was for Job:

> For I know that my Redeemer lives, and at the last He will stand upon the earth. And after my skin has been thus destroyed, yet in my flesh I shall see God. (Job 19:25–26)

Through Jesus Christ, Your Son, our Lord. Amen.

HYMN: "JESUS, LEAD THOU ON" (*LSB* 718)

CHAPTER 2

SHAME, GUILT, AND FEAR

This chapter will examine aspects of shame, guilt, and fear that are often present in having a miscarriage or losing an infant. We will explore further the social aspects of having lost a child.

VERSE FOR MEDITATION

But God chose what is foolish in the world to shame the wise; God chose what is weak in the world to shame the strong.

1 Corinthians 1:27

INTRODUCTION

When medical reports show no conclusive results for a miscarriage, a woman can feel afraid for her future of childbearing and ashamed that maybe she did something to cause it or didn't do something that she should have to prevent whatever caused her miscarriage. When birth announcements pour in, a grieving mother can feel guilty for not being able to rejoice with others over their happy news. When conversations in the workplace center around families and children, a bereaved mother might feel ashamed that the only contribution she is able to think to add evokes awkward silences and pitying stares.

Shame, guilt, and fear are products of the fall into sin. We have continually been lying to ourselves ever since Satan first reared his nasty head in the garden and fed Eve a mouthful of lies. Often when we are grieving, shame, guilt, and fear manifest themselves when in reality there is no reason for these feelings at all. These feelings come from the lies the world tells us, the lies we tell ourselves, and irrational ways of thinking and perceiving the world while we deal with the grief of having lost a child.

In the reproductive arena of grief due to miscarriage, stillbirth, or infant death, there is a facet of infant loss that has less to do with loss and more with never having. How can you grieve what you never had? Most of the time, losing a child is unexplainable and devastating in the medical arena. However, in some cases, infant loss can be the result of a chronic medical condition or one-time problem, which brings another level of grief, shame, and guilt with it. Some mothers may have success getting pregnant but later miscarry. In addition to having something physically wrong with her body, when experiencing miscarriage after miscarriage, she may have to live with the heartbreaking reality that she may never be able to carry a child to term. It is as if God, nature, and her own body are yelling down on her, "Shame, shame, shame!"

Most mothers who have lost a child in the womb struggle with this shame and guilt that becomes even more jabbing when the topic of children comes up. Questions about children can seem harmless enough, but her reaction to the questions and the residual effects of it can become toxic to her emotional health. The prying questions of others, such as "When are you going to start having children?" can cause a woman to face the unanswered questions about barrenness or loss that she has already been asking of herself and of God. She may feel she has already wrestled with God and no longer has the strength of will, body, and mind to wrestle with the same questions from her well-meaning family and friends. She may decide to shut the world out, lock herself up, or use the questions as fuel for the lies she has been living on in the midst of her grieving.

When asked if she has plans to have children, a woman who has miscarried can respond in one of three ways:

- "Well, that really isn't any of your business." This can be awkward and rude.
- "We had a miscarriage, and I am still healing from that." Again, that can be awkward.

- "Well, we hope to." This is the more acceptable, open-ended, and ambiguous answer.

Another dreaded question for the mother who has lost a child is "How many children do you have?" To this, she can answer in one of two ways:

- with the truth: "We lost a baby to miscarriage"; or
- with a lie, to avoid social discomfort: "None" (or give the number of living children and make no mention of those lost to miscarriage or infant death).

When questioned, a woman dealing with infant loss, miscarriage, or infertility pauses to decide how she is going to respond and to gauge how the person asking the question will react. She shoulders the responsibility of delicately navigating whether she will open up and share her grief and risk being embarrassed or remain silent for the comfort and ease of relationships and social situations.

In recent years, North American society has been moving toward removing shame from society. There are movements to force acceptance and "coexistence" upon a diverse people. The political battle cry in the United States is that there is no shame in however you want to define yourself or in whatever labels you want to attach to yourself. So why then is there so much shame, guilt, and fear when someone says something like "I am a mother of four, but one is no longer living"? Or why does a woman feel so ashamed that her nest is still empty after ten years of marriage? In such a progressive society, I wonder: Where is the shame, guilt, and fear of miscarriage, infant loss, and infertility coming from? As Christians, we can know that who we are and our life stories are based upon something stronger than a self-selected identity. If we believe and even protest that children are indeed God-given upon conception, then let us remove fear, shame, and guilt when we remember them and talk of them.

The following reflection is from mother, wife, and deaconess Melissa DeGroot. She reflects on what Mother's Day means for the mother who lost or can't have any more children.

On Secondary Infertility
and Our "Small, Dumb Family"

The sun shone brightly and cut through the brisk dawn—a welcome change from the spring doldrums of dark clouds and bitter rain. The tulips in our front yard seemed to be smiling wide open to greet the glorious morning. To say everyone had been waiting for this weather would be an understatement. Culminating such vitamin-D bliss, it was Mother's Day.

I awoke early—Knox woke me up, I should say—which enabled us to make it to church for 9 a.m. (a rarity). Members bustled about as beams of sunlight were cast through the stained glass onto each matriarch, and greetings of "Happy Mother's Day" flooded the sanctuary before service. And rightly so. I got caught up in the cheer and blessing that this day awarded me as well.

Yet I've learned not to elaborate beyond the simple "Happy Mother's Day" well-wish.

"Aw, your first Mother's Day! How special!" were the greetings directed toward me. "What a memorable day this must be for you!"

All I could do was smile and receive their kindnesses. People were coming from all directions. There simply wasn't time to explain that this wasn't my first Mother's Day. I mean, what else could I do?

"Well, I actually found out I was pregnant last Mother's Day. Oh, and the Mother's Day before that, I had miscarried just days beforehand. So, technically, this is not my first . . ."

Buzz. Kill.

The decorum was such that complex conversations were out of the question. I graciously accepted their joy over Knox. To get into the nitty-gritty details would have been awkward and out of place. And yet, a part of me felt guilty about neglecting the life that inhabited me two years ago, even if it was for only five weeks.

What troubles me even more is that even as I write this, I more often dismiss than lament that first child because I do have Knox. Please don't misunderstand me—the first pregnancy was simply a different experience from my second. Since I didn't go through the morning sickness or the pains of labor and delivery and hold that life in my arms, the physicality of that first pregnancy is a distant memory. And yet, because I now know what is involved in carrying a child and delivering it into this world, I sometimes mourn what could have been. Two precious children.

Fast-forward a few years, and my lament has changed faces.

One of the great lessons we will learn forever is that because of God, we are enough for Him. Our pious hopes and dreams do not merit our salvation, and thanks be to God for that. Which is to say, our prayers for more children do not go unheard. It's just that, throughout life, we come to learn that God wants more for us than whether we have more children.

Our son (who at the time was four and a half) asked me to pray one night that God would give him a brother or sister. *What a beautiful petition*, I thought. But I had to speak honestly with him. "God is the Author of life, and He may or may not give us more children, dear." What followed were tears and cries of "But Mommy, I'm so lonely! All my friends have brothers and sisters! I want us to be like the Brown family who have five kids! Our family is so small and dumb!"

For all the reasons one might think, this innocent and rebellious lament cut me to the quick. My husband and I desire more children too. And seeing our son in pain and being unable to do anything about it (that we haven't already ethically tried to do), has been heart-wrenching. You've all heard it before. We're among the many stable, Christian families that could provide a warm haven for more little souls, but for reasons unknown to us, our Lord has withheld this.

My human, sinful side grows weary, angry, bitter, and sad at times that with each passing year, my body becomes less likely to conceive. Also, our son grows older and more affected by the loneliness and the increasingly remote possibility of having a sibling he would be close in age to, as he is now seven. My husband's vocation as a missionary makes it difficult, both practically and financially, to consider adoption or foster care. It feels like we have tried everything. But we know that our prayers and cries have not gone unheard. The answer, however, at this time is no.

Our culture is not used to hearing no. I sure don't like it. An unholy anxiety creeps up in me that distrusts our Lord's provision. At times, my dreams appear to matter more than the reality that has been given. Inevitably, putting faith in a fantasy, false guilt kicks in—"I can't provide for my son!" I was thinking of having a child as if it were a commodity or somehow the answer to our needs as a family, rather than recognizing our souls' (both mine and my son's) needs for Jesus, love, and care. Also, false guilt told me that I was not providing for my son by giving him the siblings he wants!

This is where the sobering line in the sand gets drawn. Yes, we know children are a blessing and heritage from the Lord. *And* our Lord knows our fears. Recognizing fear is cause for repentance in itself, since our Lord is continually admonishing us not to have it. Further, God's Word is continually reminding me that we have done everything necessary, both for our son and in our marriage. Our bringing Knox to the waters of Holy Baptism is where God signed, sealed, and delivered him from eternal loneliness. Teaching him about the theology of suffering and the many crosses and blessings we bear as God's children is a holy and fulfilling vocation.

Ironically, in these darkest moments, recognizing a cross is where I often find the most comfort, knowing above all else—especially above myself—that God knows what we need, what we can handle, and that even in the midst of our longing, His grace is sufficient for our small, dumb family.

The floodgates of grace seem to burst wide open when the Word of truth indelibly reminds me, too, that not only is God's grace for me, it is for all those I love (and those I should love more), where all who believe in Jesus will never be alone, and that we are really all one big, beloved family.

God's Word reminds me that the number of people in a family or church has nothing to do with us at all—ask any pastor of a small, dying congregation—but *more,* it has everything to do with faith and God's grace that abounds.

Shame, guilt, and fear have a funny way of working their way into the smallest aspects of life, giving additional meaning to the idiom "the devil is in the details." There is protocol for navigating life, but the Miss Manners handbook doesn't exactly cover the etiquette of talking about my miscarriage or lost child or the children I still hope to have after so many miscarriages. It is a shame that a mother silently grieves the loss of her pregnancy of five weeks because, socially, women are advised by doctors not to tell anyone they are pregnant until they are twelve weeks along. It is a shame that a mother awkwardly smiles when asked how many children she has and she responds quite simply, "Two living," subtly referencing the child whose funeral was one short year ago.

Shame, guilt, and fear are not feelings that should or have to be associated with the loss of an infant or the lack of children. Nevertheless, those emotions are present and are damaging to the mother.

THREE WAYS SHAME, GUILT, AND FEAR CAN MANIFEST THEMSELVES AT THE LOSS OF A CHILD

1. **Isolation.** Shame and guilt may result when a mother who has lost a child starts to identify conflicting feelings like joy and anger toward a new mother in her circle of friends, or excitement and resentment at incoming birth announcements and baby shower invitations. These feelings can overwhelm her mentally and physically. The shame, guilt, and fear she feels may make it difficult to interact with others, leading her to believe it is better for her to isolate or retreat until the emotions subside. Unfortunately, shame, guilt, and fear may not disappear over time.

2. **Silence.** Shame and fear may cause a person to refrain from discussing aspects of a miscarriage or infant loss that might cause others to feel uncomfortable. The mother might not talk at all.

3. **Doubt.** Shame, guilt, and fear over a miscarriage or infant loss can cause a person to question whether it is acceptable to acknowledge the life she grew to love no matter how short or long the time given. A woman may doubt herself in social situations; she may question if her feelings are valid, or she may even begin to doubt her worth as an individual.

Scripture Discussion and Reflection

One of the very first indications that life had changed in Paradise for Adam and Eve was the presence of guilt and shame. Shame, guilt, and fear are emotions that I feel acutely anytime my body does not work as it is supposed to, particularly in miscarriage or in childbirth. I feel shame for not having the most cared-for and fit body, guilt for not being able to care for myself, and fear because I can't just make my body do whatever I want it to do, when I need it to do it. Often labor is described as one of the most beautiful miracles of life. When you take away the miracle of life, however, we are left with just broken and exposed bodies.

I sobbed and apologized to my husband when I was not able to bring our daughter into this world naturally. I hyperventilated about how I didn't want to have an emergency cesarean. My body was supposed to be able to bring our daughter into the world without being sliced open in an emergency cesarean. I was stripped of my clothes in a foreign country's socialized health care system, leaving me feeling exposed and embarrassed. I recall crying in the same way as I bled and bled, unable to keep our first child in my womb and sustain her life. This feeling of shame is a sign that something went very wrong along the way. It is the siren for sin and the message that this is not at all how God intended life to be.

Take a look at Genesis 3:1–11:

> Now the serpent was more crafty than any other beast of the field that the LORD God had made.
>
> He said to the woman, "Did God actually say, 'You shall not eat of any tree in the garden'?" And the woman said to the serpent, "We may eat of the fruit of the trees in the garden, but God said, 'You shall not eat of the fruit of the tree that is in the midst of the garden, neither shall you touch it, lest you die.'" But the serpent said to the woman, "You will not surely die. For God knows that when you eat of it your eyes will be opened, and you will be like God,

knowing good and evil." So when the woman saw that the tree was good for food, and that it was a delight to the eyes, and that the tree was to be desired to make one wise, she took of its fruit and ate, and she also gave some to her husband who was with her, and he ate. Then the eyes of both were opened, and they knew that they were naked. And they sewed fig leaves together and made themselves loincloths.

And they heard the sound of the LORD God walking in the garden in the cool of the day, and the man and his wife hid themselves from the presence of the LORD God among the trees of the garden. But the LORD God called to the man and said to him, "Where are you?" And he said, "I heard the sound of You in the garden, and I was afraid, because I was naked, and I hid myself." He said, "Who told you that you were naked? Have you eaten of the tree of which I commanded you not to eat?"

1.   What was the very first mistake the woman made in this text?

2.   What caused her to realize that she was naked?

People may try to comfort those who have had a miscarriage by saying, "We don't know why God allowed this, but it was His will and we just have to trust Him." If you have heard those words somewhere on your journey with grief, then I am sorry. While God does allow our children to die, just as He gives and takes away, it was never His plan that we should suffer in this way. God never intended that we should know pain, death, shame, and sadness. In the beginning, God created us to be perfect. Then sin opened our eyes, and we saw our own nakedness. God's only plan was for us to be in eternal fellowship with Him. But our new outlook on life was one of eternal damnation, so God, who never forsakes us, reversed the curse with a plan of salvation in order that we might return to the perfect state we once held in the Garden of Eden.

3.   In Genesis 3:21, the story continues for Adam and Eve, and God

does not leave them in shame and nakedness: "And the Lord God made for Adam and for his wife garments of skins and clothed them." What promise of a future plan for salvation does this action hold for Adam and Eve? Can you think of other instances in the Bible where we see the importance of God covering someone's shame?

Throughout His ministry, through His acts of healing and proclamations of hope, Jesus addressed the physical shame and embarrassment that came as a result of our sinful, broken world.

Read Mark 5:21–34 in your Bible.

Based on Jewish law, as we see in Leviticus 15:19–31, a woman with a flow of blood was considered unclean: "If a woman has a discharge of blood for many days, not at the time of her menstrual impurity, or if she has a discharge beyond the time of her impurity, all the days of the discharge she shall continue in uncleanness" (v. 25). This means that the woman in our text from Mark would have had to constantly clean and bathe herself of impurity, and that she had been doing so for twelve years. It also means that by simply touching Jesus, she would have made Him unclean as well.

In Leviticus 15:31, we read, "Thus you shall keep the people of Israel separate from their uncleanness, lest they die in their uncleanness by defiling My tabernacle that is in their midst." For the woman in Mark, this meant isolation and separation from her people and from the temple. To obtain a better understanding of the Jewish law the woman in the text from Mark would have been very familiar with, take time to read all of Leviticus 15:19–31.

4. Given the brief explanation of the implications of the Jewish law for the woman with a flow of blood for twelve years, how might shame, guilt, and fear have been manifested in her daily life? (Refer to "Three Ways Shame, Guilt, and Fear Can Manifest Themselves at the Loss of a Child" listed earlier in our study to help answer this question.)

Isolation:

Silence:

Doubt:

5. What actions of the woman with a flow of blood for twelve years might be considered "shameless" acts of faith?

Christ touched the unclean and healed them. The laws about uncleanness existed as a means to protect people not only from themselves but also from a holy and righteous God. The uncleanness of the body brought shame upon a person and cut him or her out or isolated the person from society. God reversed this and granted access to Himself through the sending of His Son.

6. How does God coming to us in flesh and blood offer a new understanding for the Jewish community with all their laws for cleanliness and uncleanliness?

Many times, we find comfort in knowing that someone shares the same shame and fears we do. We are comforted by taking counsel with other people who struggle with life's same problems. God the Son took upon Himself the greatest shame a Jewish man could take upon Himself: being crucified, naked, bloody, and unclean, cast outside the city gates to die among thieves and strangers.

7. Read Isaiah 53:3–5; then read Romans 5:1–6 and consider this: How does knowing that God knows our shame help eliminate the effects shame can have on our life?

8. What is God's answer to the shame we may feel as a result of miscarriage, infant loss, or infertility?

Personal Reflection

1. What are some aspects of your grief in which you can identify feeling ashamed?

2. Are there ways you have isolated or guarded yourself from the outside world?

3. Are there ways you have kept silent when you could have pushed yourself to talk?

4. Are there ways you began to doubt yourself and your worthiness to have children?

5. How can you challenge feelings of shame, guilt, and fear in your life?

HOMEWORK

Take time to read and reflect on "The Cobra Has Missed," a sermon for the funeral of James Joseph Keller by Pastor Hans Fiene (beginning on p. 157). Identify how Christ's victory over sin and death is not just for your child but also for you as He covers your shame, guilt, and fear with His sacrifice.

PRAYER

Gracious heavenly Father, by the sacrifice of Your Son, we obtain grace and confidence to stand upon this earth as Your children whom You have purchased and won with the holy innocent sufferings and death of Your beloved Son, Jesus Christ. Help us to let go of shame, guilt, and fear that we carry with us as a result of sin and of the very personal experiences of loss that we know. Make us bold and certain of all the blessings You have promised and given to us through Your Son. Through Jesus Christ, Your Son, our Lord. Amen.

HYMN: "A LAMB GOES UNCOMPLAINING FORTH" (*LSB* 438)

CHAPTER 3

LIVING WITH GRIEF:
HOW I WILL REMEMBER MY CHILD

This chapter explores how a miscarriage brings grief as a constant companion that we may learn to live with by acknowledging it through ritual.

VERSE FOR MEDITATION

Yet You are He who took me from the womb; You made me trust You at my mother's breasts. On You was I cast from my birth, and from my mother's womb You have been my God.

Psalm 22:9–10

INTRODUCTION

There are times when we feel we have changed so much that we look for new ways to express and commemorate that change. Other times, we look to familiar things for comfort and security and to keep us grounded. For this journey, we will acknowledge how our lives have changed due to the loss of a child by revisiting traditions, rituals, and roads. Instead of trying to fill old wineskins with new wine,[2] we will learn to look with new eyes at what we already know. We will challenge our understanding of worship and why we do what we do, while looking at how ritual was established in the Old Testament. It is my hope that through this study, a well-worn pew will become a nest of restoration and security, and a hymn once sung with lightness of heart

---

2   "Neither is new wine put into old wineskins. If it is, the skins burst and the wine is spilled and the skins are destroyed. But new wine is put into fresh wineskins, and so both are preserved." (Matthew 9:17)

will become the soul's expression of grief and comfort in time of need. This chapter will reflect on how rituals can become the rope we cling to when we are submerged in grief and how we don't have to look further than the Church to find rituals that will help us in our time of despair. We will examine ritual as something we do repeatedly to give meaning and movement to our life.

Ritual is often associated with religion. The Church has many rituals and many rites within those rituals that have significant meaning and movement. Many times we remain unaware of the practical applications and meanings of those rituals and rites. Let's think of ritual as something that God gives us and not something we create or re-create to fit our lives. The premise of this study examines ritual as it relates to basic, already-present aspects of worship and remembrance.

The following reflection is from Rebecca Kearney, a mother of four daughters, one of whom has been entrusted to the care of Christ in heaven. Her reflection explores the role of ritual in her time of grief at the loss of her second daughter.

Autopilot or Ritual

In the days following Hannah's birth, I put on the bravest face I could muster, though it was the one that cried behind my sunglasses dozens of times a day and the one that hung heavy in the palms of my hands as I stayed in the shower for an extra twenty minutes. It didn't feel very brave at the time, but looking back, I can see that it was a broken braveness and that I was pushing myself toward normalcy. In essence, the airplane of my life was badly damaged and flying on autopilot.

Before I was even pregnant with Hannah, we made plans as a family to go to San Diego for my dad's seventieth birthday. And so, for better or worse, we did go, just one day later than we had planned. I wasn't certain that the trip was a good idea, but the alternative was to stay home and wallow in the emptiness of my womb and our house without a newborn, and that seemed even more miserable than lugging my postpartum body around a hot and crowded summertime destination. So we went—my husband, our daughter, Quinn, and my parents. Somehow you *just keep going.*

Many of our family and friends had learned of Hannah's birth and passing, and during those early days after our loss, my phone continued to buzz with texts expressing thoughts and prayers from nearly everyone we knew. I couldn't respond though. I gratefully received each one, but the numbness inside wouldn't allow me to reach back. I just wanted to be away from home forever. I knew that returning home would prove to be the most difficult. But I couldn't put it off.

So a week before I was supposed to go back to work, while we were still on vacation, I called my principal, Leslie, to tell her that I just couldn't return. Not yet. School would be starting in two short weeks, and the faculty and staff were kicking off the year with mixers and meetings. In previous years, the start of the school year was my favorite event; it was better than Christmas and almost as good as Easter. If you are a teacher or love school like I always have, you know how magical those first days of a school year can be. This year, however, dread and depression stifled any excitement I had for my classes, students, and colleagues.

I sat on a bench outside a bakery where we were buying a birthday cake for my dad and cried on the phone to Leslie. She was the first person I talked to about reneging on my responsibilities as a teacher. This went against everything I *usually* stand for. I explained to her that I just wasn't ready—returning to teaching was 100 percent impossible for me.

"I'll put something together for you to share with the faculty and staff about Hannah, about my absence," I told her. "I would be grateful if you could read it to them. But I can't come back yet. I hope you understand."

Leslie encouraged me to try to come back on Friday the following week for our faculty worship time. She said it might be healing for me. All I could envision were awkward, pitiful stares from my colleagues, but I said I would think about it.

As for vacation, the time in San Diego was truly a time of joy as we celebrated my dad and relished our oldest daughter. She seemed even more beautiful in those days of deep grief. I clung to her, probably more than I should have, but our little earthly family of three was bound together even more tightly now. *I truly believe in my core that the Lord always gives us goodness amidst our sorrow—we just have to choose to see it.*

Even though there was an undercurrent of sadness that flows throughout those memories, I'm grateful we have them. I'm more grateful that my brave brokenness propelled me back from vacation and to that faculty meeting that following Friday. *You just keep putting one foot in front of the other and pray when those tears start welling.*

My dear friend and teaching partner promised to act as my bodyguard of sorts the day I returned. She had experienced loss in the form of a miscarriage several years before and vowed to protect my fragile self as I came back to work. She understood some of the pain I was experiencing. She was a gift to me during those days; even her loss had become a gift. *I am always grateful that our grief never returns to us unused for God's good. Never.*

Truly, I threw myself back into work that morning. I was not broken, or so I told myself, as I walked in through the same doors I had left by a few weeks earlier, when Hannah was growing in my womb. There were so many preparations to make before the school year began, and the distraction of it all was therapeutic in many ways.

There were dozens of cards and several vases of flowers on my desk in my classroom. I cherished those. I realize some bereaved mothers don't care for flowers, but I've always loved them—in joy and in sorrow. I didn't allow cards and flowers to make me weepy though; I showed only the brave face that day and worked among them as I made my plans for my students. A few of my dearest colleagues came to work with me. We didn't say much; we didn't need to—that's just the way with some people. I welcomed their healing presence.

Later that morning, it was time to gather for our faculty worship service. During the sermon, our campus pastor shared about his own significant health struggles during the previous spring and his road to recovery. It was hard to listen to the debilitating and life-altering circumstances he had been given, but I understood. *All the things we would never choose for ourselves* . . . He had experienced weeks of sorrow and grief, and he said that the only thing that sustained him was *prayer*. I knew that to be true as well. Then the tears started welling.

Prayer: this beautiful ritual that God has given to His people for times of laud and lament. We need to be a people who pray—for our families, for ourselves, and for others.

In our theater where this service was held, I sat in my usual spot—front row, just in front of an aisle. On this particular morning, it would prove to be a place of healing where my colleagues could minister to me. We collectively received Communion—as if that didn't take my breath away. The Lord has a way of stripping away our facade to make us authentically broken for His good and His purpose. He often does this through His rituals like Holy Communion. There is such beauty in that truth.

We quietly sang hymns as everyone received the body and blood of Jesus; I don't recall now which hymns, but if I were to guess, "How Great Thou Art" and "Great Is Thy Faithfulness" are likely choices. As row after row went forward for Communion, people passed my seat to receive the Sacrament. I lost count of the hands that reached out to squeeze mine; many people leaned over to embrace me in a comforting hug; a few even whispered in my ear, "I've lost a baby too."

By the grace of God, I was pulled close in a holy ritual that morning while the Spirit of God resided in our hearts. I was blessed by it and forever changed.

Ultimately in these most hopeless times, we are sustained by ritual. We keep going because of a community that gives life and hope. We press forward because of God's grace and goodness, even when we feel overwhelmed to the point of defeat. It is our deepest sorrow that can become the most beautiful offering to our good God.

As Rebecca's story illustrates, ritual is a way of returning to normal. Ritual helps us in times of hopelessness and sustains us for the road of grief ahead. For some who have lost a child, one of the first things we may look to do is preserve the life we had before through some sort of ritual. As noble as some ways of remembering a child may be—such as releasing balloons or donating toys to the local hospital in the name of the child—these actions do very little to sustain the memory of the child lost and return the parent to normal. These actions can assuage the pain in the moment, but they do not fill the void with something more meaningful apart from goodwill. In this chapter, we will examine how ritual was used in the Bible and also how to understand it in our grieving, as Rebecca did.

Three Ways Rituals Help Us

1. **Rituals give identity.** What we repeatedly do says something about who we are.

2. **Rituals give testimony.** What we repeatedly give attention to shows what or who is important to us—that is, God, family, self. They tell a story of where we have been.

3. **Rituals help our mind and body walk through grief.** Grieving has stages and patterns, just like ritual. Even when we can't really process what is going on, the body can repeat and act out a ritual while the mind has time to catch up.

SCRIPTURE DISCUSSION AND REFLECTION

Rituals play a significant role in religious life and in our everyday lives as well. From the little things we do that become our daily rituals to the milestone events of life, like birthdays and anniversaries, rituals help us define who we are and what is important to us. What sorts of rituals do we see in the Bible, and what purpose do they serve?

Read Exodus 12:1–28.

1. According to this reading, what makes a ritual, and what is the difference between a rite and a ritual?

2. Exodus 12 establishes the ritual of Passover. What was the purpose of this first Passover before it became a ritual?

Take some time to reflect on what the potential nature and mood of this ritual (or "rite," as used in v. 24) was for the very first Passover. Recall Exodus 1, where we see Pharaoh attempting to murder all the infant males born to the Hebrew women, first by demanding that the midwives kill them, and later, by having them drowned in the Nile River. Think of how the history of the Hebrew people might have affected the celebration and understanding of Passover for them.

3. In the event of a miscarriage, dates are remembered and often filled with some sort of reminder or ritual for the parents. Due dates come and go; delivery dates and birthdays turn into funerals or secularized celebrations of life. But all too often these dates go unnoticed and forgotten by family and friends. What is the significance of the time that Passover was supposed to mark? (Refer specifically to Exodus 12:2.)

4. Dr. John Kleinig, a theologian, writes that "rituals integrate people with each other in a community so that they can cooperate and share with each other. You can see these most obviously in the function of family meals and the importance of the Lord's Supper in your congregation."[3] With this in mind, what purpose was there in repeating the Passover?

In Exodus 12, we see where Passover finds its beginnings. Next, we see it established by God as a ritual.

Read Deuteronomy 16:1–8.

5. What is unique about Deuteronomy and how God instructs His people to go about observing the Passover? (Take note where "God" and "the LORD your God" are used, and fill in the key words in the passage below to help note the difference.)

Observe the month of Abib and keep the Passover ____ the LORD your God, for in the month of Abib the LORD your God brought you out of Egypt by night. And you shall offer the Passover sacrifice ____ the LORD your God, from the flock or the herd, at the place that the LORD _____ _____, ___ _____ _____ _____ _____ _____. You shall eat no leavened bread with it. Seven days you shall eat it with unleavened bread, the bread of affliction— for you came out of the land of Egypt in haste—that all the days of your life you may _____ _____ _____ when you came out of the land of Egypt. No leaven shall be seen with you in all your territory for seven days, nor shall any of the flesh that you sacrifice on the evening of the first day remain all night until morning. You may not offer the Passover sacrifice within any of your towns that the LORD your God _____ _____ _____, but at the place that the LORD your God _____ _____, to make _____ _____ _____ _____ _____, there you shall offer the Passover sacrifice, in the evening at sunset, at the time you came

---

3 Kleinig, "Rituals and the Enactment of the Gospel," *For the Life of the World*, 9.

out of Egypt. And you shall cook it and eat it at the place that the
LORD your God _____ _____. And in the morning you shall
turn and go to your tents. For six days you shall eat unleavened
bread, and on the seventh day there shall be a solemn assembly
_____ _____ _____ _____ _____. You shall do no work
on it.

6. Sometimes it can be tempting to establish rituals that place our
    children as the focus of what we do and why we do it. How does
    participating in rituals that hold God at the center help when
    grieving the loss of a child? (Recall Dr. Kleinig's comment about
    the purpose of ritual.)

In Deuteronomy 5:3, we read, "Not with our fathers did the LORD
make this covenant, but with us, who are all of us here alive today."
With these words, we are reminded that the observance of the Passover was handed down from generation to generation. This is clearly
illustrated in Exodus 12:24, where God commands, "You shall observe
this rite as a statute for you and for your sons forever." The rituals and
the rites within the rituals we observe in our worship today are also
handed down from generation to generation. We participate in these
timeless holy rites and rituals not out of respect for the past but for
their meaning to us in the present. The liturgy reminds us of the gifts
God has given His people throughout time, and the Sacrament points
us to the cross and Christ crucified and sustains us in our faith, especially in times of grief.

Passover was an important ritual in the Jewish community. As a
Jew, Jesus would have observed this ritual many times throughout His
earthly life. The last Passover meal He observed is one that we remember every time we celebrate the Sacrament of Holy Communion. Having reflected on the nature and mood of the very first Passover, let's do
the same with Christ's celebration of the Passover meal with His disciples. Think about what this ritual would have meant for the disciples
and how it might have differed for Christ, knowing what was waiting
for Him shortly thereafter.

7. Read Luke 22:7–20. Here we see Christ fulfilling what was prom-
    ised in Exodus 12 (deliverance not only from earthly oppressive
    rulers but, more important, from sins). Why is this fulfillment
    important today as we grieve the loss of a child?

Through Holy Communion, Christ offers us union not only with
Himself but with our brothers and sisters in Christ as well. Christ's
participation and command to take and share in the giving and receiving of forgiveness of sins makes this rite all the more significant as we
seek something to hold onto after the loss of our little one's life. Christ
binds Himself to bread and wine and physically gives Himself to us as
comfort and reassurance of His goodness and mercy. Although it may
feel as though our loss has left us empty-handed, Christ reminds us of
another truth and promise through the giving and sharing of His body
and blood: we are not empty-handed, we are not forsaken, and we have
hope of salvation in Christ. We are also reminded in Isaiah 53:4 of how
Christ shares in our griefs and sorrows: "Surely He has borne our griefs
and carried our sorrows; yet we esteemed Him stricken, smitten by
God, and afflicted."

Read Psalm 22. This is a prophetic psalm that reminds us that
Christ truly knows what it means to be abandoned and left alone in
death. His words from the cross "My God, My God, why have You
forsaken Me?" (Matthew 27:46) are not just a call to remember Psalm
22; they are an honest cry of total abandonment. The Son of God, fully
man yet fully God, died in our place so we would not have to know
that abandonment. His life, death, and participation in the rites and
rituals of life add meaning to all the rituals we are called to share where
His name is present. We remember Psalm 22 every Holy Week when
we observe the suffering and death of our Lord. It has become a ritual
in some churches to read through Psalm 22 while stripping the altar.

8. Christ, a teacher and the Son of God, would have known all the Psalms. A Jewish boy would have been very familiar with the Psalms as they were read in the synagogue. Why would Christ draw attention to Psalm 22 while He was dying on the cross? (Think on the third point regarding how rituals help in times of grieving.)

9. How does reflecting on Christ and His suffering as a part of ritual become helpful while grieving the loss of a child? Read 2 Corinthians 1:3–6 below to help you in your understanding and answer.

> Blessed be the God and Father of our Lord Jesus Christ, the Father of mercies and God of all comfort, who comforts us in all our affliction, so that we may be able to comfort those who are in any affliction, with the comfort with which we ourselves are comforted by God. For as we share abundantly in Christ's sufferings, so through Christ we share abundantly in comfort too. If we are afflicted, it is for your comfort and salvation; and if we are comforted, it is for your comfort, which you experience when you patiently endure the same sufferings that we suffer.

We also need to remember that it was not just Christ's participation in the rites and rituals but His institution of them. While His participation gives us an example to look to, His institution of the rites and rituals that we share today (namely Holy Communion and Baptism) are of even greater comfort and consolation for us because they promise us His presence, life, and salvation.

10. If we understand a rite to be the marking within a ritual that signifies the changing of a person from one status of being into another—for example, Baptism, confirmation, or marriage—then why would a rite such as Holy Communion become an important practice after having lost a child?

PERSONAL REFLECTION

We have many secular rituals in our daily lives, from brushing our teeth in a specific way at a regular time to putting up the Christmas tree in Advent. With the loss of a child, we may unwittingly create rituals without meaning or purpose as a way to help us move through grief. For example, a ritual may start by going into what would have been our child's nursery and rocking oneself to sleep through tears of grief. It may be something more corporate and intentional, like "paying it forward" at the local coffee shop in the name of your child on what was to be his or her birthday.

1. What rituals can you identify that you have incorporated into your life since the loss of your child?

2. What purpose do those rituals serve?

3. Identify how some rituals have been helpful or hurtful for you in your grieving.

4. How can you incorporate ritual to help you in your grieving? (Recall the three ways in which ritual helps.)

HOMEWORK, HYMN, AND PRAYER

This week, try incorporating into your life a God-centered ritual that helps you in your grieving process. Try using the "Remembrance Service for Family Devotion" (beginning on p. 147) once a week. You can modify it to fit your needs by changing the Bible reading, prayer, or hymn to ones you find comforting or fitting for your family.

CHAPTER 4

LIMINAL LIVING: UNDERSTANDING WHO I AM AFTER A MISCARRIAGE

This chapter explores how miscarriage challenges a woman's identity, and it seeks to give concrete answers about who she is in light of her changed status and constant identity in Christ. Topics for study are vocation, Christian identity, and liminal living.

VERSE FOR MEDITATION

Because he holds fast to Me in love, I will deliver him; I will protect him, because he knows My name. When he calls to Me, I will answer him; I will be with him in trouble; I will rescue him and honor him.

Psalm 91:14–15

INTRODUCTION

For this study, it is important to define how the words *identity, vocation, status,* and *liminal* will be used. These words will be seemingly interchangeable at times, but the words and their meanings are very different. Take a look at the definitions below and return to them as needed to maintain clarity throughout the study.

Identity

This refers to various characteristics that make up a person (e.g., nationality, family, interests, personality). These are things that aren't so easily changed and are intrinsically connected to the individual.

Vocation

This is used in reference to a calling that God has placed upon an individual that gives praise to Him through the living out of that vocation. It includes being a mother, father, teacher, doctor, lawyer, and so on.

Status

This is understood as something that is communicated and given by man, and it can change throughout one's life. It refers to a general state of being. This includes job position, being single or married, citizenship, and more.

Liminal

This is the paradoxical state of being between statuses, neither here nor there, yet in both places at the same time. This can be in reference to our heavenly citizenship, by which we have residency in heaven while still living on the earth. This can also refer to being a mother or father to a child that is no longer living.

The loss of a child brings with it many emotions, including emptiness, confusion, and a sense of having lost time, life, and identity. The arms that were once ready and waiting to hold a newborn baby are empty. The waiting in anticipation has turned into nothingness. There may be a baby room set up to receive a small bundle of life that perhaps never took his or her first breath. Maternal instincts develop from the first signs of conception; a woman begins to think not only of her wants and needs but of those of the child growing inside her. Her body bears signs of the life she is carrying. Only four weeks into a pregnancy, a woman can start to experience sore breasts, bloating, fatigue, and nausea. When that life is no more, does she stop being maternal? Should she change what would have been the baby's room into a craft or exercise room and just "move on," or save it and dare to hope of having another child in the future? Does she avoid confronting and talking about her hopes and dreams of being a mother for the child she lost because she is afraid of acknowledging that she is not who she had hoped to be?

The void a miscarriage leaves can cause a woman to feel emptied of who she is, depressed, and lost in who she was preparing to become, forgetting who she once was. Knowing who we are in Christ and in our daily vocations helps provide an anchor to which we may attach ourselves and our identity. The storms of grief will come, but the One to whom we tether ourselves is unchangeable, unbreakable. Only He provides the strength we can cling to and in which we find a foundation for existence in times of uncertainty. While a miscarriage or death of a child can leave a woman shattered in a million pieces, Christ puts her back together, offers her a lifeline to which she can hold while trying to understand who she is in light of her changed status (not a change of identity or vocation).

My husband and I were walking along the beach the day after Father's Day. More than eight months pregnant, I struggled to keep up with him as he walked and rambled on about all the "Happy 'almost' Father's Day" wishes he had received. People refused to simply leave it at "Happy Father's Day" since his baby hadn't yet been born. Frustrated, he posed this question: "At what point does a man or woman become a father or mother?" He paused for a moment and declared with great certainty, "I *am* a father! *Right now!*"

I was thrilled to hear him speak so passionately, and I responded, "Yes, you are a father!" I could have left it at that, but I went on to say, "Even if something happens and our baby dies, you would still be a father!"

He paused for a moment and looked down at the sand. I had killed his moment of joy with my observation. His walk slowed a bit, and he said, more subdued, "It's interesting, isn't it?" and the conversation just dropped. It was a possibility my husband was not ready to admit: that he could have the *identity* of father but be robbed of the chance to live out his *status* as a father. Statuses will change, but *vocation* and *identity* are given or called by God.

This time his identity of being a father was more real to him than it had been before. Ultrasounds showed much more than they did when I was only ten weeks along. For him, this baby was much more real than the first two had been. He was beginning to allow himself to embrace being a father and to recognize that his responsibilities were beginning even before our child had taken her first breath. For me, I was in awe of the changes my body was experiencing and how it was communicating that I would have a baby in less than a month. I couldn't believe that my long-awaited dream of becoming a mother was coming true. Even as my body started to reject the pregnancy, I felt the helpless responsibility of protecting the life inside of me. I wanted so much to be a mother, and I wept when someone who knew about my miscarriage would acknowledge me as a mother.

Just as pregnancy becomes the liminal state of parenthood, so does living without that child after he or she has stopped breathing. The question is, does physically having a child in hand make you a mother or father, or does the identity and vocation exist by nature of the individual and who God has called her or him to be?

In a world so desperate to redefine what is naturally communicated about identity—age, gender, race, and so forth—we find a whole class of men and women unsure whether they are able to declare themselves parents to children not living in this world. Does a woman who chooses not to have a child go back to not being a mother by making the choice to remove the child from her womb? Likewise, what about the woman who wanted to be a mother and did not choose to remove the child from her womb? One of the hardest things for me to digest in a personal medical report was the term "spontaneous abortion." It was never my choice to abort my child; it was placed upon me, and that one word changed how I felt about myself as a mother. What kind of "mother" could I be with the words "spontaneous abortion" showing up in my medical history? Words and feelings began to govern how I identified myself rather than what I knew of the identity God had already placed upon me.

The point is that our status does not change our fundamental identity or God-given vocation. A person's age, gender, and race do not change based on their status. Likewise, a man or woman does not become more of a father or mother based on the number of children he or she does or doesn't have. If it is believed that life begins at conception, then when God grants life in the womb, He also bestows vocation upon the mother and father, even if that life is taken away.

The following reflection is provided by wife and mother Kendra Voss. She reflects on what it meant for her to hold firmly onto her baptismal identity while struggling with the social ambiguities that miscarriage and infant loss have upon that identity.

FAMILY STATUS

For the first few years of my marriage, my husband was finishing his studies as a pastor, and we moved from the seminary to vicarage, back to the seminary, and then on to his first call. Living in a new place and meeting new people all the time, the question gets asked often: "Do you have any children?" After our first miscarriage, I did not know how to respond. Sometimes I shook my head no; sometimes I would say, "Not yet." I regret these responses. Our child, even though he lived only nine weeks in utero, was a child! He was a gift from God, and his short life should be celebrated! Our second child was stillborn at twenty-three weeks, and we had a funeral service and interment for her. After that, I began answering that question with, "Yes, we have two babies we will meet in heaven."

When we recognize that life begins at conception rather than birth, we acknowledge that the vocation of motherhood begins also at conception and doesn't end even if the child dies. I continue to recognize my vocation as a mother by speaking of my children and rejoicing that I will get to meet them one day!

In our three years of marriage before we were given the gift of children, I struggled with calling my husband and me a "family." Our culture talks about a family as a mom, a dad, and a child or children. But when we look to Adam and Eve, we see that God gave them to each other for companionship. He gave them to each other to be helpers to tend the Garden of Eden. He then gave them the gift of children using their companionship of marriage (sex). They were not incomplete before their children. They were complete as husband and wife. Once we found out I was pregnant, it finally felt like I could call us a family, but I had lost sight of the relationship God had given me in my husband. I coveted more, even though I had already been given more than I deserved.

Because I had lost sight of the wonderful gift that is my husband, when we lost our precious babies, it felt like we had lost our status as "family." But the truth is that when our babies died, we did not lose our identity or our status as "family"; we are still husband and wife, still one flesh, still a family.

When I found out I was pregnant, I noticed that my personality and my interests changed almost instantly. Suddenly, I began researching baby cribs and nursery themes. I went window shopping with friends who gave me their opinions on baby products. I put together a registry of items we would need for our baby. I was doing all these things instead of pursuing my other interests, and I was excited about it. It consumed my time; rarely was there a moment that I wasn't thinking about the child who was growing in my womb.

When we lost our baby, my mind turned away from all of those thoughts. I no longer obsessed about what room would be the nursery, what color scheme we would go with. However, my old interests never returned to my mind either. I used to love bowling and photography and playing my trombone, but those things don't hold my interest anymore. Since my heart and my mind are trying to forget all the planning I did for our baby and I'm no longer interested in the things I used to be, I feel lost; my identity feels lost.

My husband said the other day that I seem sad all the time. I am sad, not just because my arms are empty, but because my interests changed during pregnancy, and I do not feel the same passion for them as I used to. I also haven't found any new passions. My body is still adjusting to not being pregnant, and at the same time it is behaving in a certain way because I did give birth. Some days I feel like I can conquer the world, and other days, all I can do is sit and watch DVDs.

When we first moved to Homestead for my husband's call, I was excited to be doing dishes and cleaning the house and doing the laundry because I was going to be staying home with the baby when she came. This was my vocation: "housewife/mother." After Ruth died, I lost that enjoyment. Doing the dishes and laundry and cleaning are chores now. They are constant reminders that I don't have a legitimate reason to stay at home without a job. When I lost my child, not only did I lose my status as "mom," I lost my status as a "stay-at-home mom."

Some days I am perfectly grounded in who I am and what my identity is, while other days I feel completely blank and lost. I am thankful for friends who continue to ask how I am doing. And I am learning to be honest. Just the other day, a friend reminded me that even though I feel as if I have lost my identity, my identity is founded in Christ. I am a baptized child of God! That does not change my vocation or identity. God claimed me as His own child in the waters of Holy Baptism on June 8, 1986. Since then, I have had a lot of vocation and identity changes. I have added "sibling," "wife," "pastor's wife," and "mother" to my vocation as "child." My status has changed to "college student," "married," and "has family," and yet during these changes, my identity has never changed. I am a child of God. Knowing this helps me in many ways. It means that I am always loved, even when I don't feel like I deserve love. It means that even on days when I fail to get the laundry or dishes done or clean the house and I feel like a failure because that's my "job," my heavenly Father still loves me. It means that when I ask for forgiveness, He offers it.

Being a child of God also means that I have a huge family that will support me and will pray for me. It means that I am never alone.

Three Ways Identity Helps

1. **Identity helps us respond in personal crisis.** Knowing who we are and what the fundamental makeup of our identity is gives us a core explanation we can go to when we are challenged in who and how we identify ourselves. When we base our identity in our Baptism, we know that other aspects that make up who we are can be challenged or taken away, but who we are in Christ remains. This grants stability when our foundation is shaken.

2. **Identity gives meaning, purpose, and direction to our life.** Knowing we are baptized children of God reminds us that our identity is not connected first and foremost to our abilities and responsibilities but to our calling in Christ Jesus. Through His calling upon our life, we understand better the meaning of our existence and direction of our life, even when it doesn't go as we planned.

3. **Identity helps to shape our worldview, which gives us a foundation from which to respond to the outside world.** Being identified as a Christian and child of God reminds us that our hope is not in things of this world but in heavenly things.

Scripture Discussion and Reflection

Where does our identity come from? This question is answered in many ways in the Bible—it comes from God, who created us in His image. Abram is a prime example of what it means to receive an identity from God and how God gives and calls us into an identity that is intimately connected to Him. Let's take a general overview of the patriarch Abram to help us in our understanding of God's communication of identity through His calling.

We start in Genesis 12:1, where we see God calling Abram and saying, "Go from your country and your kindred and your father's house to the land that I will show you." From the beginning, we see God calling Abram from various identifying agents for him: country, kindred, house, and land.

Next, in Genesis 15:1–6, we see God claiming Abram as a chosen leader and father for a people set apart for God and as a recipient of a whole new land, family, and life in general: "Fear not, Abram, I am your shield; your reward shall be very great" (v. 1). In verse 5, God tells Abram who He will make him to be—a father of many. God says, "'Look toward heaven, and number the stars, if you are able to number them.' Then He said to him, 'So shall your offspring be.'"

In Genesis 17:1–8, God changes Abram's name to Abraham and again promises him, "You shall be the father of a multitude of nations. No longer shall your name be called Abram, but your name shall be Abraham, for I have made you the father of a multitude of nations. I will make you exceedingly fruitful, and I will make you into nations, and kings shall come from you" (vv. 4–6).

Continue by reading Genesis 22:1–19.

1. How is Abraham a perfect example of someone who finds identity in God?

2. How does God challenge Abraham in the identity that God laid out for him in asking him to sacrifice his only son?

3. What are some of the specific things that Abraham says that display his trust in God throughout the narrative?

Verse 6 says, "Abraham took the wood of the burnt offering and laid it on Isaac his son." We can't say for sure that Abraham knew beforehand that God was only testing him, but some theologians say that his response in verse 5—"I and the boy will go over there and worship and come again to you"—indicates that Abraham believed that even if he had to kill his son, the Lord would raise him to life again. So Abraham willingly placed the wood upon Isaac's back and climbed Mount Moriah to sacrifice his only son. This event closely resembles the Passion of Christ, when God the Father sent His only Son, who carried the wood of the cross upon His back up the hill of Golgotha, and who then rose to life. The difference, of course, is that our Savior did become the ultimate sacrifice in His death.

4. If God is not a God who desires human sacrifice, and He is a God who already knows the hearts and minds of His people, what is the purpose of testing Abraham in this way?

5. God promised Abraham yet again after testing him that he would be blessed and his offspring would be multiplied. Yet, Abraham had only two sons. Knowing the fulfillment of God's promise to Abraham, what can we conclude about God's calling and God's timing? (Think of what liminal living means.)

To God, Abraham was the father of many and a reference point when He addressed His people: "'I am the God of Abraham, and the God of Isaac, and the God of Jacob' . . . He is not God of the dead, but of the living" (Matthew 22:32).

6. How does having a God who identifies Himself with a broken people become a comfort to a mother or father who has lost a child?

Perhaps you do not feel as though you are struggling with your identity in Christ, or maybe you do not struggle with worshiping God despite your loss of status as a mother. Continue to take time to daily renew your sense of identity in Christ. It is important to continue to cling to all that Christ offers us and to remember that in Christ, there is no loss of identity but rather a gaining. All is gain, even though at times it may be difficult to grasp. Christ gives us all that He is through the water and Word of Holy Baptism, and when we cling to His promises poured out over us, we find a better identity to cling to. We can find meaning and purpose, and in the midst of the loss of life, we can find direction to move forward after the heart of our beloved little one has stopped. We find that our worldview is no longer limited to this earthly life alone. Instead we hold the strong assurance of new life in Christ, just as our baby is entrusted to His care. In our personal crisis, we find Christ as our rock and cornerstone to cling to and trust, just as we read in Acts 17:28—"in Him we live and move and have our being." In Christ, we have already been renewed in the waters of Holy Baptism and have put on a new identity.

How do we know that even without our child living in this life our identity as mother or father has not changed?

> But standing by the cross of Jesus were His mother and His mother's sister, Mary the wife of Clopas, and Mary Magdalene. When Jesus saw His mother and the disciple whom He loved standing nearby, He said to His mother, "Woman, behold, your son!" Then He said to the disciple, "Behold, your mother!" And from that hour the disciple took her to his own home. (John 19:25–27)

7. Why do you think John recorded the event of Jesus giving Mary and His "beloved disciple" to be mother and son to each other in the midst of His death and dying? More important, why did He address the replacement of His mother's son from the cross?

Christ's earthly ministry not only acknowledges our human need for vocation with a status, but it also identifies our need for identity. Through Baptism, we are given a new identity that we can cling to at all times, especially in times of crisis. When we struggle with who we are, we remember that we are first and foremost a child of God. No matter how broken we feel, Christ offers us unity, freedom, and the promise of resurrection by giving us His own identity to cling to.

> Do you not know that all of us who have been baptized into Christ Jesus were baptized into His death? We were buried therefore with Him by baptism into death, in order that, just as Christ was raised from the dead by the glory of the Father, we too might walk in newness of life.
>
> For if we have been united with Him in a death like His, we shall certainly be united with Him in a resurrection like His. We know that our old self was crucified with Him in order that the body of sin might be brought to nothing, so that we would no longer be enslaved to sin. For one who has died has been set free from sin. Now if we have died with Christ, we believe that we will also live with Him. We know that Christ, being raised from the dead, will never die again; death no longer has dominion over Him. (Romans 6:3–9)

8. Our status as mother changes when we lose a child, but our identity as mother does not change. How does having Christ as the foundation of our identity solidify our identity as mother even in the midst of having lost a child?

9. Recall the first three words defined earlier: *identity*, *vocation*, and *status*. Why is it important to distinguish among them when trying to understand what it is you lost and who you are in the context of your loss?

10. Based on the definitions of those words, who defines an individual's identity, vocation, and status?

11. How is a secularized identity different from an identity based in Christ?

12. How does our Baptism support liminal living for us in the midst of grief, and what hope does liminal living offer you?

PERSONAL REFLECTION

1. How have you seen your identity challenged in the midst of your loss?

2. Take a look again at the three points in which identity can help. How had you hoped your identity as a mother might be fulfilled in each point?

3. How can you continue to recognize the vocation of being a mother that God has given you while living without your child?

HOMEWORK

Read Psalm 91. Take time to reflect on it and think about the comfort found in the promises of holding God as the center of your identity. In your journal, write what the evidence is of one who trusts in God, and what various promises are offered for those who find their identity in God.

PRAYER

Gracious heavenly Father, You called us to be parents to *("the life You gave us" or insert the name of your child)* for such a short time. Help us to remember that while we continue to be a mother and father without our child, our most important calling was poured out over us in Baptism. Keep us focused on Your Son and the gifts You daily and richly pour out over us through His sacrifice for us. We thank You for the gift of salvation that we cling to more and more with each passing day as we learn what it means to be Your child. Guard our hearts and minds in You, through Jesus Christ, Your Son, our Lord. Amen.

HYMN: "GOD'S OWN CHILD, I GLADLY SAY IT" (*LSB* 594)

CHAPTER 5

LEARNING TO TALK ABOUT MY LOSS

This chapter will explore what comforts can be found in sharing the story of your miscarriage or infant loss with others. We will also explore how sharing one's grief can give better understanding of our integration into the story of salvation. Topics for study will be telling the story, the Christian's pilgrimage, and participation in the sufferings of the cross.

VERSE FOR MEDITATION

You have kept count of my tossings; put my tears in Your bottle. Are they not in Your book?

Psalm 56:8

INTRODUCTION

I worked as a chaplain student in Cambridge, England, during a study abroad. In our training, we were told that people want to talk, and it would be our task to draw the story out of the patients we engaged with. During the visits I made, I discovered that I seldom had to do much drawing out. Most of the people I visited freely offered up the details of their lives: regrets; dreams; details of surgery, illness, or condition; details about past and present relationships; what their family was like—just about anything. It was rare for me to visit the same person more than once, which might be why they felt free to share such intimate details with me. I would go home at night with a head full of stories of people from a culture different from what I was familiar with. Their stories became a beautiful tapestry within my mind of that time spent away from home. I still have in my Bible some of the notes I made reminding me how I could pray for some of the patients throughout the week. I felt, during the minutes and hours I spent at their bedsides, that I was brought into their life to ponder whatever it was they chose to share. It was an honor and a privilege to be entrusted with the details, the memories, and the struggles.

As I read my Bible throughout the years, the stories therein shared something as equally beautiful as the stories of my patients in England. All the stories in the Bible point to Christ with artistry that we could not invent through the stories alone. Likewise, the stories of our own lives also point to God. In sharing fellowship in Christ, we share a pilgrimage with fellow sojourners. My mind's eye sees it as a beautiful quilt with shapes and stitches carefully binding each piece of fabric to the next. Better yet, I see a woven piece of fabric where individual threads come together as a whole to make one larger design that tells a story. It's as if we are all woven into the cross, sharing burdens and joys as we are integrated into the same story.

The story of loss may be as simple as telling someone "I lost my baby," while allowing the silence and the tears to fill the void and communicate the rest. Telling the story of your loss might also be more like what my patients in Cambridge did, spilling their own details in an unexpected moment. Your loss is a part of who you are. And like those people in that Cambridge hospital, when you share the details of loss, you invite people to come alongside you on the pilgrimage of faith, joy, suffering, contemplation, and participation in the sufferings of Christ. As we set off on our shared journey, we share also in the joining together as a quilt or woven tapestry that tells a story, not as an individual thread but as a collective whole. Where Christ walked the road of suffering on our behalf, we are ourselves connected to Him on that same road. Yet we are not alone, and sharing our stories not only provides an outlet for understanding the struggles of our brothers and sisters in Christ, but also binds us in deeper communion with Christ and His sufferings on the cross.

It is a blessing to be able to tell of the lives short-lived in and out of the womb. It can be healing to hear and say their names out loud. It does a mother good to hear how God loved her little one. I recall being reluctant to share my story of loss, thinking and feeling that it was insignificant in comparison with the losses of others. Later, I wept when one of the women I shared my story with acknowledged the life I lost and, what was more, connected that life to God by saying, "God loves you, and He loves your child." More than wanting to tell my story of loss, I wanted to know that what I had lost was connected to the greater story of salvation, because only therein would I not have lost but gained a child in Christ.

Following is the story of Kristen Gregory. She reflects on the life of her daughter given to her more than ten years ago. She shares what has become important to her in recalling the life of her little girl.

"HOW MANY CHILDREN DO YOU HAVE?"

It's a fair question but a complicated one. I always hesitate before I answer. I take a moment to size up the person and situation first. The reality is, I have been pregnant eleven times, but I have four living children. So how much do I want to go into with a stranger?

If I answer, "Five," I've decided this person seems safe enough, and I share with her the story of Vivian Anastasia, our daughter who lived almost six months before she went home.

To our great joy, we had gotten pregnant on our honeymoon, and our lives felt so full and happy. We were carefree and confident. When I went for my normal prenatal checkup on January 31, 2008, I had no idea what that evening held for me. I was thirty-three weeks pregnant and was measuring small, so my midwife recommended I get an ultrasound. We didn't have maternity insurance (we were young, healthy, and poor), so I hadn't had one yet.

Every year since, January 31 is a day I dread as the anniversary of the single most terrifying experience of my life. Throughout the entire ultrasound, the technician was silent. We had no inkling anything was amiss until I noticed all the office staff hustling around, looking at our room, whispering. When the doctor came into the room, she appeared extremely serious, and she said, "I have you scheduled for a C-section in an hour." We were speechless.

"Wait, I don't understand." I wasn't having contractions. I wasn't in labor. I was a nanny, and I had two kids sitting on my lap who weren't even mine. What was I supposed to do with them?

"Your baby is measuring under two pounds. The placenta is deteriorating. I don't know what is wrong, but we need to get the baby out right now."

"Is the baby going to die?"

"I don't know. It could. We need to operate now." I suddenly felt very detached from my body. Everything had been fine that morning; my world had been perfect that morning. My husband burst into tears.

Somehow, we made our way to the operating room. It was cold, so unbearably cold, and I was in such shock that I was shaking violently. The room was silent as the doctor cut and pulled. I saw my blood spurt up and hit her glasses. "Is everything okay? Can someone tell me what is going on? Do you see the baby?" I asked. Silence. Peter and I tried to pray the psalm we had memorized in preparation for labor, but we were so shaken we could only remember a few words.

Finally, a barely audible cry. "It's a girl," someone announced. The NICU doctor took over, put our unnamed daughter in a clear box, and began to wheel her away, hand-bagging her lungs.

"Wait," my husband said. "It's important for Kristen to see her." They stopped for a split-second, and I glimpsed her dark eyes and black hair. Would she still be alive when they finished stitching me up? Every ounce of maternal instinct in me wanted to cry out, "Give me my baby!"

As the staff finished operating on me, we decided on a name so we could baptize her as soon as she was stabilized. Knowing that she might die soon and that she had been due on Easter, we named her Vivian Anastasia, which means "the resurrection and the life." I lay in the recovery room alone while my child was baptized with sterile water and an eyedropper.

My two-pound-three-ounce daughter didn't die that night, to the surprise of the staff. I lay in my bed, angry and depressed and in pain. We were allowed into the NICU every three hours to see her, but I couldn't gather the courage. All the tubes and wires and alarms. We weren't allowed to touch her. Why connect with her if she was just going to die? I'll never forget the wisdom and strength of my husband at that time. He wept as he said, "If this is the only time I have with her, then I want to get to know her while I can." And he dragged his tired body across the hall every three hours to see his daughter.

It didn't take long for me to put aside my despair and join him. That weekend, the hospital was moving from a three-bed NICU to a facility with individual rooms, and we were the first patients transferred to the new unit. We had no idea it would be our home for the next 168 days. As I recovered, my desire to mother Vivian grew, and so did my heartache at being unable to comfort her. We constantly sang hymns and read Scripture to her, but she was in such critical condition that we couldn't even pick her up. Finally, a nurse arranged to let me do "kangaroo care"—chest to chest—and the relief it brought both me and Vivian was immediately evident. Her vitals improved drastically as she lay in my arms. But it was also a huge ordeal—it required a nurse and a respiratory therapist to remove and reconnect her ventilator, and a four- to eight-hour time commitment on my part during which I couldn't move because her wires and tubes were taped in place on me.

About that time, I was still trying to make sense of Vivian's traumatic birth. I decided to walk back through the operating room, but when I visited that unit, it was gone. It was a construction zone; the hospital was remodeling that area. That was a big blow to processing my grief. Years later, I requested my hospital files from the doctor, which were helpful, but the absence of a physical location was still upsetting to me.

Slowly, Vivian's oxygen needs were decreasing and the doctors started talking about her going home in March or April. We were feeding her fortified breast milk through a nasogastric tube every three hours (breast- and bottle-feeding didn't work since she had a cleft palate and was ventilated), but she wasn't growing. A geneticist was brought in to run tests on her, and in mid-April, she was diagnosed with a rare dwarfism called Russell-Silver syndrome. Most babies with that condition are small and have a hard time eating, but Vivian's case was severe. It led to surgeries to place a G-tube in her belly and tie off the opening of her stomach so she wouldn't regurgitate all her food. After that surgery, our hopes of bringing her home disintegrated. She developed pneumonia after pneumonia, had lung damage from the ventilation, had heart damage from the lung damage, and so on.

Peter and I slept together on the couch next to Vivian's bed in the NICU most of those nights. We woke constantly to the sounds of alarms and to emergencies and slept very poorly.

Since we had been blessed with this pregnancy in the first month of our marriage and she had been born early, we were in many ways still getting to know each other. How were we supposed to talk about the impending death of our child? His response was so different from mine, and I was frustrated because I expected him to have the same emotions as I did. And we tend to take out our anger on those nearest to us. The nurses watched as our ability to communicate broke down rapidly. The rate of divorce in situations like ours is phenomenal, and we started going to counseling to salvage our relationship and learn to cope with the huge emotions.

Over those months, Vivian almost died many times. I saw the staff assigned to her reading the protocol about death. Blood sugars of four hundred. Profuse sweating. Increased diuretics. Highest-pressure ventilators, yet oxygen levels dropped lower and lower. We wrote out our own protocol of what to pray over her if she died without us present. I rarely felt comfortable going to church—or leaving the hospital for any reason—because I was terrified that she would die alone. I literally ran every time I used the bathroom across the hall for fear she would die when I was out of the room.

On July 16, she ran a high fever but was very awake and alert. We took many pictures of her smiling, making eye contact with people, and looking at her favorite stuffed animal. We felt free enough to go back to our house four miles away and swim in our landlord's pool. It was a great gift to our marriage and the first thing we had done together in almost six months besides keep vigil at Vivian's bed.

The next day, Vivian still had a high fever and her oxygen level was 30 percent. Her skin was grayish and sweaty, and she never opened her eyes. We all knew death couldn't be far away, but no one said it openly. The doctor stopped doing daily blood draws, and we had a no-resuscitation plan in place.

I held her in the early afternoon and then passed her off to our primary nurse, who had never held her before. I noticed her eyes were red, and she had been crying. Then Peter stepped in and held Vivian for the first time in weeks. As he was holding her, the heart monitor changed from sharp spikes to a wavy line. "This is it," I remember calling out. The nurse turned off the monitor so we could focus on our last few seconds with our daughter. We automatically started praying the Lord's Prayer over her, and her eyes flickered open for the first time that day. By the end of the prayer, her eyes closed again forever. She went directly from the arms of her earthly father to those of her heavenly Father. It was 6:56 p.m. Peter removed her tracheal tube, and we took out all the wires and tubes and, for the first time in her life, held her freely.

I had no idea how I would feel holding my dead child, even though I had imagined it plenty of times. To be honest, there was a sense of relief after so many months of waiting for her death. I'm not sure I even cried that night. The lump in my throat and constantly racing heartbeat finally vanished. I took the first deep breath I could muster in twenty-four weeks.

But just because your child dies, that doesn't mean the maternal instinct can easily be put to death. I couldn't imagine just leaving her body at the hospital. Who would take her? Would they be gentle and kind with her body? The staff didn't rush us; we stayed at the hospital another eight hours and put her on the couch between us so we could pretend to be a normal family, just once.

Peter was exhausted and finally asked if we could go home. We reluctantly placed her body in the care of two nurses, who slowly and gently walked down the hall with her to meet the undertaker. It was one of the most painful moments of my life.

We drove home and fell into bed. And I honestly don't remember much of the next year. I know I wasn't able to fall asleep before 3 a.m. for months because sleep would bring nightmares. My husband tells me I would wake up in a panic, frantically searching the bed for our daughter. I had an irresistible desire to take care of her, but she wasn't here to take care of.

After Vivian died, I felt so aimless. I had quit my job to stay home with her, and now it was just me home alone with my grief—which was itself like a full-time job. When I went grocery shopping, I felt strange going alone, so I carried the scrapbooks I had made in the NICU in the front of the cart. I needed proof that I was a mother.

I'm not a crier, but I cried constantly. My eyes were swollen for months. Church was brutal. I believed what I heard, but it was so painful and fresh that I just sat and listened. I couldn't sing the hymns, often couldn't say the prayers, couldn't even stand up. I just absorbed it and wept.

Our marriage was awkward at first. It took at least half a year before I stopped crying every time we made love; I felt guilty for being happy and enjoying something when my daughter's cold body was decaying in the ground. Peter was working a new job from sunup to well after sundown, so I was processing almost everything on my own. I had to wrestle with God—just me and Him. I had come into marriage thinking that if we were obedient to God—waiting to be together until we were married and being open to children—life would be smooth and seamless. It still is a daily struggle to have faith that Christ is the promise and gift God gives all Christians, and not motherhood or anything else. He is sufficient, even in the midst of suffering.

Since Vivian died, I have had five miscarriages. Five years after her death, we had a son in the same NICU with most of the same staff. Lazarus— aptly named before we knew anything was wrong—was misdiagnosed as having an infection, but it turned out that he had several severe heart defects. He was immediately airlifted to a children's hospital two hours away, which saved his life but took us on a similar journey, where we had to revisit our fears of losing a child and trusting that God is always good to His children.

Throughout Vivian's hospital stay, we daily read Psalm 27. "I believe that I shall look upon the goodness of the LORD in the land of the living" (v. 13) was a promise we wanted her to hear and we needed to hear ourselves. It's etched on her tombstone. I hope that everyone who sees it is reminded that God is good and the next life with Him is worth suffering for.

One doesn't easily adjust from an intense half-year hospital stay to a normal life. At first, I visited the NICU weekly. Then, as time wore on and more babies came, we visited monthly, and then only on her birthday and death date. Then we moved across the country, and we haven't visited in three years.

Faithful friends and family members propped us up at that time. They asked about Vivian; they sent cards for years on her birthday and death day, just letting us know that she was a part of their lives too, and that they loved us and her. As time goes on, people have tended to forget her special dates, but I've let go of that and have been comforted by the fact that it doesn't matter that other people don't always remember her—God has always loved her fiercely and will never forget her. As my home gets fuller with each child and I forget some of the details of Vivian's life—what her voice sounded like, how she smelled—I know I am not betraying her. If I develop dementia in my old age and can't remember her, God remembers it all.

How comforting to know that her value doesn't come from what I make of her; her value comes from being a child of God.

How Telling the Story Can Be Helpful

1. **It allows others to know how to help.** When you can share with others the struggles of your miscarriage, it helps them to know how to pray and how to help. It is always important to notify your pastor so he knows and so he can prompt the whole congregation to pray and help.

2. **It helps us see how we are integrated into the larger story of salvation.** Sometimes when we share our story of grief, others' stories of grief also surface and we realize that we are not alone. Our Savior's own story of His Passion and suffering shows us this and reminds us how He calls to us in our pain to draw us closer to Him.

3. **It can be cathartic for some to share the details of the life they lost.** For verbal processors, telling the story is a way of working through what has happened, and it is a way to help understand the loss of a child more deeply. It is also a way of making sense of feelings, emotions, and struggles that have never been felt at such a magnitude before.

Scripture Discussion and Reflection

The Bible tells one of the most wonderful stories, that of our salvation. Not all the stories in the Scriptures are nice and leave you with warm fuzzy feelings. They are, however, stories of a people saved by God that give testimony to His saving works. Not only can it be validating for an individual to tell a story; it sometimes can also surface with details and revelations of how God has been present and working and pointing us to salvation through Christ Jesus.

As we saw in the chapter on ritual (starting on p. 42), Hebrew culture was founded on the story of a people saved by God. They told their story of salvation through oral tradition. For Jews, their daily lives and their identity as a people of God were intimately intertwined as a community. Our lives look much different today; many people prefer solitude over intimacy. We tend to be private and separated from others. We have professional personas we try to maintain, and we keep our issues close to the chest where they can't be seen so we can't be judged by them. In some cultures, grief is often exhibited publicly and corporately. But other cultures choose to grieve in private silence, especially when it comes to miscarriage. We can see in the Bible that in Jewish culture, there was no such thing as personal privacy. Consider the times Christ tried to withdraw from the crowds, only to be surrounded by a multitude of people. Let's take a look at the account of one woman and how her story can help us share our stories with others.

In Luke, we see an excellent example of storytelling. Read the verses below, and focus on the context surrounding them.

> And all who heard it wondered at what the shepherds told them. But Mary treasured up all these things, pondering them in her heart. And the shepherds returned, glorifying and praising God for all they had heard and seen, as it had been told them. (Luke 2:18–20)

> And they did not understand the saying that He spoke to them. And He went down with them and came to Nazareth and was submissive to them. And His mother treasured up all these

things in her heart.

And Jesus increased in wisdom and in stature and in favor with God and man. (Luke 2:50–52)

1. A reference is made in Luke 2:19 and repeated in Luke 2:51: Mary "treasured up all these things, pondering them in her heart." The accounts in Luke 3 then switch to Christ's adult life. What are these references pointing to, and what can be concluded from them?

2. Speculating that Luke gathered his information for the writing of his Gospel after the death and resurrection of Christ, what more might Mary have been pondering and treasuring in her heart as she recalled the birth of her Son and shared it with Luke?

Dr. Arthur Just explains in his commentary on Luke that Mary "carried this holy child for nine months and raised him as her son. She heard the word and then kept that word by cherishing it in her heart and trusting it. The 'fulfillment for the things spoken to her by the Lord' (1:45) would ultimately pierce her soul with a sword (2:35) when she witnessed her Son's crucifixion. But she was there also on the third day. God would keep her in the faith."[4]

3. Of all the things Mary witnessed and treasured in her heart—the birth, life, death, and resurrection of her Son—it is easy to imagine that witnessing His death could have tainted all her wonderful memories of being His mother, as it says it pierced "her soul with a sword." Why would it become so important that Mary give attention not only to the horrific manner in which her Son died, but also to the details she had treasured up in her heart, such as His birth and childhood?

Throughout all of Luke, we see a pattern of "hearing" or "seeing" and then "sharing," and all the details point to Christ. Details aren't just important for good and accurate storytelling; they are important

---

4   Just, *Luke 1:1–9:50*, Concordia Commentary, 77.

for showing concern and value. Details make the story personal. God places a lot of importance on details to show His care for us, as we can see in the Verse for Meditation:

You have kept count of my tossings; put my tears in Your bottle.
Are they not in Your book? (Psalm 56:8)

While Mary pondered and treasured the details of her Son's birth and death in her heart, God records the details of our lives, right down to each tear shed. The details of your life are important to God, and so are the details of your child's life. This is demonstrated in various parts of the Bible, such as Luke 12:7: "Why, even the hairs of your head are all numbered. Fear not; you are of more value than many sparrows." The amazing thing about the details of our lives is that they don't just tell a story; they point to Christ or lead us to Christ and open our eyes to see Christ all the more clearly.

While Mary was pondering all the details of her Son's birth and death, she was also pondering God made flesh among us. It is certain that in light of His resurrection, she pondered her life as mother to the Son of God with new eyes. This was a perspective that her younger self, even as an innocent child, understood perfectly well and responded to with faithfulness: "Let it be to me according to your word" (Luke 1:38). Mary knew and, with faith like a child's, she trusted that God would bring about the salvation of His people through the Child who was within her. All the details of her history as a Jewish woman pointed this out to be true.

Take a look at the Magnificat, which Mary sang after being greeted by Elizabeth.

And Mary said,

"My soul magnifies the Lord, and my spirit rejoices in God my Savior, for He has looked on the humble estate of His servant. For behold, from now on all generations will call me blessed; for He who is mighty has done great things for me, and holy is His name. And His mercy is for those who fear Him from generation to generation. He has shown strength with His arm; He has scattered the proud in the thoughts of their hearts; He has brought down the mighty from their thrones and exalted those of humble estate; He has filled the hungry with good things, and the rich He has sent away empty. He has helped His servant Israel, in remembrance of His mercy, as He spoke to our fathers, to Abraham and to His offspring forever."

And Mary remained with her about three months and returned to her home. (Luke 1:46–56)

The Magnificat is a beautiful canticle that we also sing in the worship service today. It gives praise to God and rejoices in all the wonderful, salvific actions He performed throughout generations. The interesting thing we see in the passage is that Mary's song of praise was not original. Her words run parallel to another song recorded in the Bible and most likely were words Mary would have sung in recounting the works of God when in the fellowship of other Jewish women.

Let's take a look at Hannah's prayer:

And Hannah prayed and said,

"My heart exults in the Lord; my horn is exalted in the Lord. My mouth derides my enemies, because I rejoice in Your salvation.

"There is none holy like the Lord: for there is none besides You; there is no rock like our God. Talk no more so very proudly, let not arrogance come from your mouth; for the Lord is a God of knowledge, and by Him actions are weighed. The bows of the mighty are broken, but the feeble bind on strength. Those who were full have hired themselves out for bread, but those who were hungry have ceased to hunger. The barren has borne seven, but she who has many children is forlorn. The Lord kills and brings to life; He brings down to Sheol and raises up. The Lord makes poor and makes rich; He brings low and He exalts. He raises up the poor from the dust; He lifts the needy from the ash heap to make them sit with princes and inherit a seat of honor.

For the pillars of the earth are the Lord's, and on them He has set the world.

"He will guard the feet of His faithful ones, but the wicked shall be cut off in darkness, for not by might shall a man prevail. The adversaries of the Lord shall be broken to pieces; against them He will thunder in heaven. The Lord will judge the ends of the earth; He will give strength to His king and exalt the horn of His anointed." (1 Samuel 2:1–10)

4. What similarities and differences do you see between Hannah's story and Mary's story?

5. How does Hannah's story become part of Mary's story and vice versa?

6. How do the Magnificat and Hannah's prayer give us an example of what it means to be incorporated into the greater story of salvation?

7. How does having lost a child bring us into the stories of both Mary and Hannah today?

Dr. Luther explains the Magnificat and Mary's purpose in singing it:

Just as a book title indicates what is the contents of the book, so this word "magnifies" is used by Mary to indicate what her hymn of praise is to be about, namely, the great works and deeds of God, for the strengthening of our faith, for the comforting of all those of low degree, and for the terrifying of all the mighty ones of earth. We are to let the hymn serve this threefold purpose; for she sang it not for herself alone but for us all, to sing it after her.[5]

It is comforting to think that even when our stories seem so distant from those others in time and detail, there is unity in the sufferings of Christ. It is because of His work on the cross that we, too, can sing

5   AE 21:306.

the songs of Mary and Hannah as if they were our own. The comfort offered to us in the loss of a child is the same that is offered to the woman who is never able to have a child. Christ, who never forsakes us, becomes our bonding agent and our only source of all comfort in times of grief.

Personal Reflection

1. What details are important to you in remembering the life of your child, and how can you share them with others? (Something to think on: Mary and Hannah shared this in song.)

2. What would you want people to know about the life of your child?

3. In the Bible discussion portion of this chapter, we identified that connection comes through Christ. Sometimes it is difficult to find the link or connection to others in the stories of loss, especially when it comes to the loss of a child who perhaps wasn't even able to be baptized. Take some time to reflect on the text from 1 Corinthians 15:54–58 and think on how knowing and clinging to Christ's story helps give deeper meaning to your own story of loss.

Homework

Take some time to write your story and see what new aspects emerge that you never noticed before in just telling it.

Prayer

Gracious heavenly Father, You brought us into Your story of salvation by sending Your Son to die for us and make a way back to You. We pray that You would help us not only to see Your salvation in our everyday lives but also in the stories of our children who have been entrusted to You. Help us to see the blessing in the fact that our stories may be unique to us but they are not unique on their own. Help us to find comfort in the greater story of salvation that is not limited to a few but is told for all. Through Your Son, Jesus Christ, our Lord. Amen.

HYMN: "MY SOUL NOW MAGNIFIES THE LORD" (*LSB* 934)

CHAPTER 6

MY PLACE IN THE BODY OF CHRIST

This chapter will challenge the way we try to help ourselves. We will seek to understand how locking ourselves up does not lock the grief out; rather, it isolates us. We will explore how to take time for ourselves to study the Word of God. And we will explore why we need the Church, even when her members seem less than helpful at times. The topic for study will be reincorporation into the Body of Christ.

VERSE FOR MEDITATION

Rejoice with those who rejoice, weep with those who weep.

Romans 12:15

INTRODUCTION

Perhaps it has been a few weeks since you last sat in the pews of your beloved church. Maybe you took some time off to grieve after your miscarriage, or maybe you felt you needed a break from church to reflect on the funeral of your child that you were too overwhelmed at the time to process. So it has been a few weeks, or even months, and now you are sitting in the same pew you sat in so many times before, only this time you feel a profound sadness as you recall that the last time you were sitting there, you were rejoicing at the prospect of sharing it with a baby. Maybe your seat brings back other memories of singing "I Am Jesus' Little Lamb" as you watched a tiny casket, light enough for one person to carry down the aisle to the front of the church. Whatever memories or hopes the place evokes for you, you choke down your tears and decide to try your best to reincorporate yourself back into the church.

You exchange fake smiles with a few members and figure that if you look through the announcements in the bulletin, people will figure you are busy or distracted. It works for a while until you come to the announcement about helping provide meals for new mothers. *I was a mother!* you think. You sit in silence, staring blankly at the announcement, contemplating how much life has changed for you and yet it just keeps rolling forward for everyone else. It is as if your world fell dark and just stopped growing, like you were taken out of a summer day and dropped into a brisk winter with no hope of spring. You push yourself forward to read more in the bulletin, hoping there might be something else to distract you. But everything makes you think of the life that is no longer with you. Everything, big and small, twists in your mind until it is about your baby. An announcement for confirmation class: *My baby would have taken confirmation.* An announcement for the church budget: *I have to pay the hospital bills from the baby.* An announcement for next Sunday's potluck dinner: *Next Sunday my baby would be twelve weeks gestation* or *My baby would be one month old.* The bulletin is no longer announcements for the church but a personal reminder that you once had a baby.

You decide to redirect your attention to the people near you again. Maybe striking up a conversation with someone might be distracting. You look around and see the Jones family, who had a baby two months ago, and you decide you aren't really in the mood to talk about their newborn, which is clearly where that conversation would go. You see the group of pregnant moms you used to participate with when you were pregnant too, and you suddenly feel sick to your stomach. Maybe it's a good time to get a drink of water or go to the bathroom. On your way to the bathroom, you see the print of Jesus with little children climbing all over Him and the verse that says, "Let the little children come to Me" inscribed at the bottom. It seems like even Jesus is pointing and saying, "Where's your child?" You make it all the way to the bathroom, which, oddly enough, is located in the same hall as the cry room and all the Sunday School classrooms for ten-year-olds and younger.

It is as if everything is calling your attention to the fact that you went to battle with childbearing and lost the child and a limb in action. You are experiencing trauma from your miscarriage or infant loss, and the church seems to be unintentionally triggering it in every way possible.

Because of that, reincorporation into the church can be difficult, delayed, or even dismissed. But it is a necessary step in the grieving process. When we are turned inward, we may fail to realize that our grieving can be deeply connected to and affected by the church; yet we desperately need the routine of worship and the church family to get through our grief. The Body of Christ is a blessing in every situation, but it can be difficult to see that when everything reminds you of what you no longer have. What once felt supportive might now seem as if it has left you hanging. How do we reincorporate ourselves back into the congregation when we feel like a broken, limbless body after the blow of losing a child?

The following reflection is from a pastor's wife and mother of four, Audrey Daenzer. She reflects on how the church embraced her in her time of grief and how beautiful and necessary her incorporation into the Body has been to her in her grieving.

Perpetua Felicity

On Ash Wednesday morning, I lay on an exam table in a dim room as the ultrasound technician told us, "I'm sorry; I can't find a heartbeat." And on Ash Wednesday evening, I knelt at the Communion rail, my heart heavy, crushed by grief and the knowledge of the tiny dead body in my womb. My pastor husband and I decided not to tell anyone at our church that night about the loss of our precious baby so as not to detract from the service. Nor did I want to stay home from church; I knew I needed to hear my Lord's words of forgiveness and comfort. Yet as person after well-meaning person asked, "How are you feeling?" and, "How many weeks along are you again?" I began to regret our decision to hide our terrible news. I feared being alone; I did not want to hide; I needed others to share in our sorrow.

The next day my husband began to call elders and other church leaders, who promptly got the phone chains going. Almost immediately, casseroles began to show up in the church refrigerator and sympathy cards slowly filled our mailbox. Even before I had a chance to speak to anyone, our members showed us that we were not alone in the midst of our grief.

Our sweet baby girl, Perpetua Felicity, was born that Saturday. She was about the size of my hand, with tiny facial features and perfect little hands and feet. We held her and loved her and cried for her; and then, eventually, we had to let her go. Saying good-bye was one of the hardest things I have ever done. As the nurse wheeled me, empty-handed, out of the maternity ward, I had never felt so numb and alone.

The next day we stayed home from church. I was still recovering physically from the induction and delivery, and the elders encouraged my husband to find a substitute pastor so he could stay home with his family. Ironically, a new little baby girl was baptized at church that morning. While I rejoiced in her new life in Christ, inwardly I was relieved that I did not have to be there to see it happen. Instead we prayed Matins at home as a family, and we sang "A Mighty Fortress Is Our God," the Hymn of the Day for the First Sunday in Lent:

> And take they our life,
> Goods, fame, child, and wife,
> Though these all be gone,
> Our vict'ry has been won;
> The Kingdom ours remaineth.

> (*LSB* 656:4)

The words that I had sung dozens of times from memory suddenly took on a new, bittersweet meaning.

My first time back in church—and first time out of the house since my induction—was at Lenten midweek Vespers a week after my ultrasound. I slipped into the empty back pew, hiding where I hoped people wouldn't see me. Before the service had even started, however, the elder on duty was hugging me and telling me how sorry he was.

We sang "Abide with Me" as the closing hymn, and I started crying during the fifth stanza:

> I fear no foe with Thee at hand to bless;
> Ills have no weight and tears no bitterness.
> Where is death's sting? Where, grave, thy victory?
> I triumph still if Thou abide with me!

(*LSB* 878:5)

By the end of the service, I was a mess, but suddenly I was surrounded by a queue of people hugging me and crying with me and telling me they were sorry and were praying for us. Two women told me of the little babies they had lost at about the same gestation as Perpetua many years ago. So much grief and sorrow, hidden for so long. Hearing of others' pregnancy losses was sad and overwhelming, but it also made me feel less alone at a time when I was terrified of being alone. In the end, while I felt terribly self-conscious and feared that people would avoid me, say something rude or insensitive, or just give me pitying glances, I was embraced with love and support. My dear fellow Christians knew what it meant to "rejoice with those who rejoice" (as they did while I was pregnant) and "mourn with those who mourn" (Romans 12:15). One member of the Body was suffering, and the other members were deeply affected in turn.

Still, my first weeks and months back in church were not easy. I woke up every Sunday morning with a sense of anxiety—it was the one time each week when I *had* to get out of the house and spend time with other people. I was still nervous that someone would say something unkind or insensitive to me, so I avoided chatting with people after the service. I wanted to talk about what had happened, to share even my daughter's name, but I didn't know how to approach the topic, so I avoided it altogether. After only a few weeks, most people stopped mentioning the miscarriage and asking how I was doing. They seemed to have forgotten and moved on, and I was afraid that I was supposed to "move on" as well, when my grief still felt new and sharp and overwhelming. I felt very alone. I strongly felt the absence of my baby as I struggled through services in the pew with my two living daughters, sometimes wondering if perhaps God had taken her because He knew I could not handle having another child. Mostly, though, I wished Perpetua could be there to hear the liturgy and sway with the hymns, just as I had rocked my other babies through service after service.

Baptisms were especially difficult. One of my favorite hymns, "God's Own Child, I Gladly Say It (I am baptized into Christ!)" (*LSB* 594:1) now felt like a slap in the face. I could not sing it without doubt and frustration creeping in. How could I rejoice in my Baptism when my own child had been unable to receive this precious gift? Witnessing the Baptisms of other children was upsetting too. I became particularly angry with the apathy of inactive parents who brought their older children to the font because it suddenly became convenient or because it was something they wanted to check off their list of "things we should probably do." How could I rejoice in the Baptism of a child whose parents would likely not darken the door of a church for another decade, when I would have given anything to raise my little daughter in the Christian faith?

Despite all my inward struggling, Christ was—and remains—merciful to me. From the beginning, our beautifully rich Lutheran hymns brought me great comfort. Sometimes I could barely sing through the tears, but the voices of my fellow believers around me continued the words when I could not:

> God gives me my days of gladness,
> And I will trust Him still
> When He sends me sadness.

God is good; His love attends me
Day by day,
Come what may,
Guides me and defends me.

(*LSB* 756:3)

The liturgy remained consistent, week after week, repeating God's promises over and over when nothing else seemed sure or constant to me anymore. I heard the Words of Absolution: "In the stead and by the command of my Lord Jesus Christ I forgive you all your sins in the name of the Father and of the Son and of the Holy Spirit." I confessed the hope of the resurrection in the Nicene Creed: "I look for the resurrection of the dead and the life of the world to come."[6] I knelt at the Communion rail, receiving my Lord's precious body and blood for the forgiveness of my sins—even those sins tied in with my grief. And I knew that at that rail I was also a part of the marriage feast of the Lamb, joining "with angels and archangels and with all the company of heaven"[7]—the whole communion of saints. I trusted and prayed that my little Perpetua Felicity was with Christ, that she had just what her name means—everlasting happiness—with her Lord. And if she was in Christ, then she was a part of that host of saints gathered around the Lamb.

The cherubim, their faces veiled from light,
While saints in wonder kneel,
Sing praise to Him whose face with glory bright
No earthly masks conceal.
This sacrament God gives us
Binds us in unity,
Joins earth with heav'n beyond us,
Time with eternity!

(*LSB* 639:3)

---

6   *LSB*, p. 191.
7   *LSB*, p. 208.

If there was any place on earth where I could be close to my baby, it was there.

Going to church can be tough, even on the best days. My preschooler squirms and whispers a little too loudly, "Are we done yet?" The toddler escapes under the pew and hides her shoe in the purse of the lady sitting in front of us. A newborn baby cries somewhere behind me, distracting me from the sermon as I think again of my empty arms and the baby I'll never get to know in this life. We sing a hymn that reminds me of a quiet burial service that's all too fresh in my memory. Everyone acts as though nothing has changed and life keeps moving on, while deep down I'm still struggling and know that nothing will ever be the same again.

But do not lose heart, dear grieving mother. Do not stay away from the church for too long. Our Lord says, "For where two or three are gathered in My name, there am I among them" (Matthew 18:20). In the Divine Service, Christ comes to you and lavishes you with His gifts in the Means of Grace. He forgives your every sin. He comforts you in your grief. He reminds you that His death has destroyed death forever, that there will be a resurrection and a life to come. He joins you to Himself in His very body and blood. He even gives you fellow Christians to sing and pray with you when you have no words to pray, to bring you a hot dish or a plate of cookies, to give you a hug or to cry with you, to mention your missing child by name. Perhaps your fellow believers do not understand your sorrow; they ignore you or make unkind comments or expect you to move on. Our Lord forgives their sins too. Perhaps you feel that you are empty and weak and have nothing to contribute to your church. Our Lord requires nothing from you. Come, hear His Word, and receive His gifts of forgiveness, life, and salvation. Be reminded of your Baptism and know that you are Christ's; nothing can snatch you out of His hand. Taste His body and blood, and know that in Him you are united with the whole Christian Church in heaven and on earth.

The Body of Christ is made up of broken sinners, it is true. Yet Christ is the Church's Head and Cornerstone. He is the center of our worship, our life, our faith. In Him, the Church is a place of comfort and healing. In the months after my loss, I sang many hymns at home with my girls. One of my favorites was "Lord Jesus Christ, the Church's Head" (*LSB* 647). It is a prayer that Christ will keep His Church and all believers faithful to the end. For it is Christ who builds His Church, and even the gates of hell—and death—will not prevail against it (Matthew 16:18).

> O Lord, let this Your little flock,
> Your name alone confessing,
> Continue in Your loving care,
> True unity possessing.
> Your sacraments, O Lord,
> And Your saving Word
> To us, Lord, pure retain.
> Grant that they may remain
> Our only strength and comfort.
>
> (*LSB* 647:2)

Sometimes it seems like the best protection plan is avoidance. In the case of miscarriage and infant loss, it might be the easiest, but it isn't the best. You will suffer and feel pain as a result of the loss, no matter what. That pain and suffering might be perpetuated by the unwitting remarks of some, the joyful pregnancies of others, and the uncomfortable avoidance of many. Cutting out these people does not protect you more from further pain; it only makes you more isolated and lost in pain. Part of the process of healing and coming to understand the suffering is suffering with others.

What You Need to Know for Reincorporation into the Body

1. **Reincorporation requires nothing of you.** Being a member of the Body means that when a member of the Body is hurting or wounded, the whole Body reacts to the wounded member to help assess and heal it. Allow people to help you. And if you are

an active member in your church, take some "time off" from activities, but don't count worship among those activities. If you are not an active member, perhaps try meeting with a pastor to let him know of your struggles; he should be able to guide you to being incorporated into the church.

2. **It will be messy.** Treat it like a marriage. If your congregation doesn't respond in a helpful way, don't give up because you don't like how the church does or doesn't do things. Talk with the pastor; talk with friends from the church, and let them know what will be most helpful for you in healing. Don't decide to stop going in order to help yourself. Take this as an opportunity to educate the church and help make things better for the next mom who loses a child and comes running for comfort.

3. **The earlier the better.** The longer you put off going to church, the less likely you are to return. It's like the medicine you keep on your nightstand: after forgetting to take it for a while, you figure you don't really need it because you don't feel any worse for not taking it. Trust that it is something you need, even if it feels better to not go.

Scripture Discussion and Reflection

There are a lot of reasons why people stop going or never start going to church, and a lot of them have to do with a misunderstanding of what the Church is supposed to be. I am guilty, as are many women, of denying help because I have fallen for the lie that I can or should be able to do everything myself; yet at the same time I complain that there is no one to help me. The Church and her members often become the object of our reasoning for not going: we don't like the sermons, we think they are a bunch of hypocrites, the pastor preaches too much Law, or the women are too fussy. With these sorts of thoughts, we must be careful because we run the risk of victimizing ourselves. When we are the victim, we can become a part of the problem and not a part of the solution. We might assume that our grief is too big or too personal for the Church to know what to do with it. Sometimes, instead of addressing the issues, we avoid the congregation, forgetting the real reason why we need her. Specifically, we need the Church because that is where we hear Christ's healing word of the Gospel, that is where we are united with Him in the waters of Baptism, and that is where He comes to us in His restorative Holy Meal. Yet we let our sinful selves get in the way. We let Satan distract us from our church.

Trouble in the local congregation is nothing new, of course. As we will read here, conflict in the Church is a main topic of many of the Epistles. Let's see what sort of help we can glean from the Epistles to better understand the role of the Church in our grief.

Take a look at Ephesians 2:20–22:

> [You are] built on the foundation of the apostles and prophets, Christ Jesus Himself being the cornerstone, in whom the whole structure, being joined together, grows into a holy temple in the Lord. In Him you also are being built together into a dwelling place for God by the Spirit.

1. Ephesians identifies the Church in three different ways. How does this text identify the Church? What are the specific words used?

2. What is the Church to be built upon, and what does this mean for the structure itself?

Read Ephesians 4:11–16:

> And He gave the apostles, the prophets, the evangelists, the shepherds and teachers, to equip the saints for the work of ministry, for building up the body of Christ, until we all attain to the unity of the faith and of the knowledge of the Son of God, to mature manhood, to the measure of the stature of the fullness of Christ, so that we may no longer be children, tossed to and fro by the waves and carried about by every wind of doctrine, by human cunning, by craftiness in deceitful schemes. Rather, speaking the truth in love, we are to grow up in every way into Him who is the head, into Christ, from whom the whole body, joined and held together by every joint with which it is equipped, when each part is working properly, makes the body grow so that it builds itself up in love.

3. To what does this text compare the Church, and what specific words are used?

4. How is the Church supposed to grow according to the above text?

In his Letter to the Romans, Paul talks further about the Church and how her members are to reflect Christ. Sometimes, thoughtless comments and careless acts can be taken as reasons to separate from the Church. Paul suggests that where there is weakness, there is also an opportunity to show mercy, and that this exchange of mercy and humility is necessary for the existence of the Church.

Read Romans 12:1–12 in your Bible.

5. Why do we also need all the Church's members, no matter how hypocritical, broken, and unhelpful they might seem to us or others?

6. How can embracing our broken selves serve us in our healing and our worship of God?

I was born with only one ear that can hear; the condition is known as "unilateral hearing." The other ear that can't hear is left on my head not only for aesthetic purposes; it also serves me in ways one would not expect. It adds equilibrium to my head. It gives me a greater appreciation for the ear that can hear and, likewise, I am thankful for the ear that can't hear when the street noise is especially loud. The weaker member of my body gives importance to the stronger member, and the stronger member appreciates the weaker member for simplifying things.

Having lost a child, we may feel like a broken shell, occupying a small space in a pew. But for the woman who has never experienced a miscarriage or loss of a child, you become the reason she holds her children closer and thanks God for each and every one of her kids, even when they are misbehaving. For the grown man who was in and out of foster care all throughout his youth, you become a reflection of what motherly love looks like in the absence of a child. We will never fully know what our own weaknesses mean for others, but we can be certain that even if it is amplified in the church, it is not in vain.

7. How can we draw other members of the church into our lives without feeling we need to cover or hide our weakness or brokenness?

Wives, submit to your own husbands, as to the Lord. For the husband is the head of the wife even as Christ is the head of the church, His body, and is Himself its Savior. Now as the church submits to Christ, so also wives should submit in everything to their husbands.

Husbands, love your wives, as Christ loved the church and gave Himself up for her, that He might sanctify her, having cleansed her by the washing of water with the word, so that He might present the church to Himself in splendor, without spot or wrinkle or any such thing, that she might be holy and without blemish. (Ephesians 5:22–27)

8. To what does Paul compare the Church in Ephesians 5, and what specific words does he use?

9. What lessons are learned in marriage that we sometimes fail to apply with the Church's members as well?

10. In each of these texts from Ephesians, how is Christ identified?

Ephesians 2:20

Ephesians 4:15

Ephesians 5:23

11. Why is it important for us to recall that Christ is the focal point and most important aspect of the Church?

12. What happens when Christ is not held as the center of worship and church activities?

Read Psalm 84 in your Bible.

13. In your own words, how does the psalmist identify the Church?

14. Sometimes in our grief, we forget why we attend worship. We think, *I have nothing to give*, and so we stop going for a time. For what reasons do we go to church?

PERSONAL REFLECTION

1. In what ways has church become a safe haven or an oasis for you in your time of grief?

2. What would your ideal church look like in her response toward a mother who just lost a child?

3. Are your expectations realistic, and if so, how can you help your present church to resemble more the church you idealized?

4. What are some things you can do to help others help you in your grief?

HOMEWORK

What were some of the specific things people in your congregation did to help you in your time of grief? Who were those specific people? How did their concern for you make you feel? Take some time to write a note to those people and let them know how they helped you feel more incorporated into the Body of Christ. Encourage them to continue in the work that they do. Maybe even invite them into your home to share some time with them and to share more intimately the details of your grief with them.

If your church was not supportive or you do not belong to a church, schedule a time to speak with a pastor and ask him to pray for you. Sometimes a church might not be as supportive as we would hope because they don't know about what has happened. Find ways to open up and share what you are grieving so that the Body will know how to react and help.

PRAYER

Gracious heavenly Father, we thank and praise You for the gift of the Church. Teach us to lean upon the Body of Christ and all her members in our time of need. Remind us of our place within the Church and the blessings to be received in hearing Your Word and receiving the Sacraments. We thank You for this nest of healing You provide for us and for bringing us safely within the arms of Your Church in our time of loss. Grant us comfort through Your Word and healing through Your Sacraments. Grant us a sense of belonging among the Church's members while we wrestle with our losses. All this we ask through Jesus Christ, Your Son, our Lord. Amen.

HYMN: "LORD JESUS CHRIST, THE CHURCH'S HEAD" (*LSB* 647)

FORGIVING OTHERS

This chapter explores some of the things people say in trying to console someone who has suffered a miscarriage or infant loss. We will also explore why it is more important to maintain a disposition of forgiveness toward others. We will also consider what our Christian obligation is in forgiving others. This study will be more about the sin and Law in grieving. The topic for study is forgiveness.

VERSE FOR MEDITATION

And forgive us our debts, as we also have forgiven our debtors.

Matthew 6:12

INTRODUCTION

The delicate state a woman is in after a miscarriage or infant loss can leave us with insatiable hunger for the Gospel. I believe that we are stronger than we give ourselves credit for, and there are times when we can and do need to hear what the Law of the Lord means for us, even in the midst of our grief. In this chapter, we will pray with the psalmist, "Open my eyes, that I may behold wondrous things out of Your law" (Psalm 119:18), and we will pray that the working of the Lord's Law upon our hearts will bring us to a place where we can see more clearly and grieve unburdened by the indiscretions of others.

People often try to comfort with indiscriminate words, platitudes, or ideas from their own invented theology of comfort when they are talking with someone who is struggling with a loss or death. Words can hurt and can be damaging to a person in the frail state of grief after a miscarriage or infant loss. There have been times when someone said something to me with the most innocent intention of helping, and I overanalyzed what they said. Hours later, after careful consideration, their words felt malicious and evil to my heavy heart. Words were twisted within my mind and caused damage.

At the same time, the lack of words can hurt just as much. It's painful when husbands remain silent for fear of saying the wrong thing to their wives while they are grieving. The silence can be taken as a lack of interest or absence of compassion. It can also be taken as though they are pretending nothing happened and are moving onward and forward. Often, we take what would be a sin of omission and we turn it into a sin of commission. When we do this, we only weigh ourselves down with the additional and unnecessary burden of thinking that others are against us in our grief. We may even begin to sin against our neighbor by harboring feelings of resentment and anger toward their careless stumbling upon our road of grief.

The key to managing reckless comments is forgiveness. Just as Christ was and is our prime example of forgiving those who sin against us, so He is our source of forgiveness as well. He not only shows how to forgive, but He freely forgives and frees us of our burden by forgiving others on our behalf and by forgiving us when we do not freely forgive. We can lean all the more heavily upon His forgiveness when forgiveness does not flow so freely from us. We can know that anger, resentment, and frustration with the cluelessness and tactlessness of others is not worth carrying around. And we can repent and know that His forgiveness will equally be freely given to us when we realize where we ourselves have fallen short in expecting other sinners to be better comforters for us in our pain.

The following is my own reflection on forgiving others in the midst of having had a miscarriage.

FATHER, FORGIVE THEM WHEN I CAN'T

I was a newlywed, in my early thirties, and married to a pastor, and our congregation as well as my husband and I were anxious to start not just a new life together but a family as well. We were living in Argentina (my husband's native land), and we were dreaming about what our children would be like and imagining our life with little ones running around our tiny apartment and filling our life with joy. Little did we know how complicated the process of becoming and staying pregnant could be, especially when under the stress of new jobs, new locations, new lives, and a new church family.

The first pregnancy test we took showed one bold line and a faint second one. We bought five more tests in our doubt, thinking surely one would work better than the other and give us the answer we wanted. I was driving my husband crazy with my baby obsession, comparing lines and tests and flipping between doubt and certainty of my status of being pregnant or not. Early on, I started to bleed, and I recall thinking, *Well, maybe this is my body's way of preparing for the real thing*. I was sad but hopeful that the next time would be more certain and it would be easier.

The next set of pregnancy tests showed two bold lines, and we couldn't believe that we were going to be parents. Our waiting wasn't long, and the joy my husband and I shared the night I took the pregnancy test felt more like a dream than our new reality. We didn't want to play around this time with tests and doubt, so we went directly to the doctor. The doctor started with a basic pregnancy test that showed up negative. I was numb, thinking that it couldn't be right, that the test must have been faulty. I knew that wasn't all there was to our baby story. The doctor sent me to have an ultrasound done to see if there was something else to explain the results of our home test and pregnancy-like symptoms. The results showed that I had a cyst.

It still didn't add up for me. I continued to take at-home pregnancy tests that continued to show up positive. When I returned to the doctor with the results from the ultrasound, I was attended by her PA and was told what I was already able to know from the ultrasound technician's notes I was handed earlier: "You have a cyst." I explained to the PA that it still didn't add up with all the positive tests I had and the symptoms I was experiencing. "I must be pregnant; there has to be some other explanation."

She consulted with the doctor to see if the doctor could give a better explanation. Through the curtain, I heard the whole conversation between the PA and the doctor, and it came as a second blow for me. Rather annoyed, the doctor said, "No! She isn't pregnant; she has a cyst. It's clear, right here. The pregnancy tests are positive for the cyst. Tell her to have the cyst removed." Her response was cold and fact based. Her form of mercy was to send me home with an aggressive three-day antibiotic to prevent any infections.

This was my first experience with socialized health care in a foreign country, and I was tired of the testing, waiting, and insensitive handling of my fragile state. My husband and I agreed that we would go to a private ob-gyn to deal with the cyst, as the public hospital had more than a months-long waiting list.

The private ob-gyn was a new doctor for me, and we had to tell him the whole story about what we had been through in the past two weeks with the hospital doctor and tests. He performed an ultrasound right there in his office and froze the screen. Triumphantly, he said, "Just as I thought! You do have a cyst that is perfectly normal within pregnancy. It is called a 'Lutetium cyst.' It accompanies the fetus and will go away after a few months. If we take out the cyst, we will terminate the pregnancy."

I was returned to my dreamlike state of joy with my husband that night as we contemplated the names we would give to our child. It was the news I wanted—I *was* pregnant. But I was so tired from all the ups and downs of thinking I was and I wasn't and then that I was again.

The new doctor scheduled us to come back for a checkup in a month. During that month, signs of pregnancy became more and more clear, and our excitement of waiting and dreaming increased. We were preparing to travel to my husband's hometown for our nephew's Baptism, our godson, and we were anxious to share the wonderful news with his family then.

We went back to the doctor the same day as our scheduled departure for the Baptism. The doctor asked me how I was feeling, and with the feel of the pregnancy glow, I responded, "Just a little tired."

However, upon examination with an ultrasound, he informed us that our baby had "failed to grow" and that I would pass the fetus in a few days.

Heartbroken, we traveled that night, and I prepared myself to "deliver" my baby in another city under the umbrella of joy for the new spiritual life given to our godson. After nearly a twenty-four-hour journey, we arrived at my husband's hometown and were greeted by his sister, with her baby in her arms.

Nobody knew how awful I was feeling, not only because of the knowledge I carried but also because of the sickening feeling of heavy bleeding and contracting that my body was going through. At first, I was saddened by my in-laws with all their questions about when we were going to start a family. I was hurt that they assumed we weren't trying and because they never asked about what our hopes were. Nobody asked me how I was doing, much less how I was feeling. People didn't seem to care about me at a very basic level.

When we returned home, a few close members of the church who knew I was making frequent visits to the doctor asked how I was doing. When I explained what happened and told them the story, their response was, "Well, at least you didn't have to have a D&C," or, "At least you weren't that far along." Others just ignored what I said altogether and changed the subject quickly.

Because I was so emotional, it took me some time to realize that their responses didn't come from a place of unsympathetic, cold indifference but rather from ignorance. Just as I learned how hard it is to share the details of an emotional journey of losing a child in the womb, it is also difficult to know how to respond to that person, let alone have just the right words she wants or needs. My husband didn't know how to help me, and church members didn't know how to respond to me. And I realized that instead of finding comfort in God's forgiveness and His Word and Sacraments, I was seeking counsel and comfort in the wrong places.

For a time, I became angry and bitter that people weren't more how I wanted and needed them to be for me. I wanted young mothers to stop having babies so my hurting heart wouldn't feel so much pain. I wanted other women to hold me and tell me that everything was going to be all right. I wanted my husband to hug me and say sweet things like "You are so strong for having to go through this."

At the very least, I wanted people to acknowledge the life most of them never even knew existed because we hadn't been far enough along in our pregnancy for us to tell them.

I realized over time that what I needed to hear was "Suck it up, buttercup!" That became my motto. It didn't mean I was pushing the grief aside; it meant I needed to forgive these people for my own sake, like it or not. I realized that I was becoming a very fragile person, and I was demanding that people stop everything to be there for me and to be who I needed them to be. I realized that those around me weren't who and what I needed most, but that also I could grieve and be strong in my grieving.

My grief made me selfish at times. My grief had become an all-consuming, unreasonable disability that placed me as the victim and everyone else as the unsympathetic attackers. I couldn't see Christ in my neighbor, and I certainly couldn't even begin to think of forgiving them.

I didn't stay the victim, though. By the Lord's leading, I realized that the power to forgive and be forgiven remained *with Christ in me*, and not in my own ability to extend and receive forgiveness. For those who said the really insensitive things, I depended even more heavily on Christ's forgiveness. When I allowed their words to penetrate my thoughts and bring back the pain of miscarriage, I would pray, "Father, forgive them for they know not what they do," and I would remind myself that whatever forgiveness flowed out of me was of Him and not of myself. I also had to remind myself that I was in just as much need of that same forgiveness for placing unrealistic expectations on people. Left alone, I wanted to just keep on blaming others for the pain I was feeling. In my mind, it wasn't just one person's fault; it was the whole country's fault. But I found peace knowing that forgiving them released me from those painful and, quite frankly, exhausting feelings of carrying resentment and anger around. Instead, I charged Christ with the burden of forgiveness.

I had to forgive doctors for careless diagnosing, family for lack of support, friends and acquaintances for careless words. And I had to ask for forgiveness for myself.

In our congregation, we practice the "passing of the peace": we kiss one another on the cheek and say, "The Lord's peace be with you." We do this right before the Lord's Supper to show that we have fellowship and peace with one another. The practice is based on Matthew 5:23–24. I learned to depend heavily on the peace God gives as opposed to the peace I could seek or find. By myself, I could not find peace, but I needed God's peace to cover myself and the offenses of others—and it does. He covers them with the blood of His Lamb, "the Lamb of God who takes away the sin of the world."

THINGS TO REMEMBER ABOUT FORGIVENESS

1. **Christ shows us how to forgive.** "But God shows His love for us in that while we were still sinners, Christ died for us" (Romans 5:8). God did not wait for us to ask for His forgiveness; He won for us forgiveness while we were still dead in our sin and before we even knew our need for forgiveness.

2. **Forgiveness flows first from God.** At times, forgiveness is not our natural practice, and we need an intercessor to do for us what we know we ought to do but are unable to.

This is where we can lean heavily upon the forgiveness God gives and know that because of Him, all sins are forgiven, even when it doesn't feel like it.

3. **Forgiveness brings deeper healing.** Holding onto anger, resentment, and hurtful grudges for words wrongfully spoken holds us captive to sin and keeps us from a right relationship not only with our neighbor but also with God. This is true even when we are the ones who have been sinned against. When we forgive, we free ourselves from unnecessary doubts and burdens. We release ourselves from whatever power wrongful words might have over us, and we obtain peace with God and our neighbor.

Scripture Discussion and Reflection

The Bible gives us many examples of how we are to conduct ourselves within the Body of Christ. We hope that others would follow biblical etiquette when one is struggling with grief. The hard part, perhaps, is that there is also biblical instruction for the one who is grieving and how she is to receive those who express less-than-comforting counsel. Again, Christ is our example in such times. Our task as faithful Christian women is to take up yet another cross in the midst of our grief. Not only do we grieve, but we must also forgive those who know not what they do. We forgive without gossiping and bringing up their social awkwardness or their indiscreet remarks within our closed groups. We forgive without trying to paint ourselves as victims and martyrs of child loss. We forgive by holding our tongue when it seems like it could be cathartic to share what one more person wrongfully said or did.

Take a look at the following text:

> And when they came to the place that is called The Skull, there they crucified Him, and the criminals, one on His right and one on His left. And Jesus said, "Father, forgive them, for they know not what they do." And they cast lots to divide His garments. And the people stood by, watching, but the rulers scoffed at Him, saying, "He saved others; let Him save Himself, if He is the Christ of God, His Chosen One!" (Luke 23:33–35)

1. Our Lord begged for the pardon for others while being nailed to the cross. What can we learn from Christ's words "Father, forgive them, for they know not what they do" as we prepare our own petitions of forgiveness?

2. What were the people doing that required forgiveness, and why didn't Christ spell out each sin He was asking the Father to forgive?

3. Why is it important for us to ask for forgiveness from the Father on behalf of others, even when they don't know of the sins they've committed?

Read the following Scripture passage:

> Put on then, as God's chosen ones, holy and beloved, compassionate hearts, kindness, humility, meekness, and patience, bearing with one another and, if one has a complaint against another, forgiving each other; as the Lord has forgiven you, so you also must forgive. And above all these put on love, which binds everything together in perfect harmony. (Colossians 3:12–14)

4. Why does Christ become an essential part of the equation when we are talking about forgiving others and living in community with one another?

Read Luke 7:36–48 in your Bible.

5. The woman in the story is an example of forgiveness primarily for the forgiveness that Christ gave her but also for the forgiveness she would have to give on a daily basis to those who knew her and talked about her. In what ways does this text show that she would be expected to forgive and to love as she had been forgiven and loved?

6. How might being given the chance to forgive Simon for his words grant a deeper healing to the sinful woman in the above text?

In the woman's shame and grief, she would not find room in her heart to be concerned with what Simon the Pharisee thought and said; she needed only to know that she was forgiven. The same goes for us as we grieve our little ones. Let us make it so that there is only space in our hearts to allow Christ to work forgiveness and healing, and no room for harboring additional pain, suffering, and grief for the careless words of others.

Create in me a clean heart, O God, and renew a right spirit within

me. Cast me not away from Your presence, and take not Your
Holy Spirit from me. Restore to me the joy of Your salvation, and
uphold me with a willing spirit.

Then I will teach transgressors Your ways, and sinners will return
to You. (Psalm 51:10–13)

7.   In the midst of grief, it is easy to be consumed with thoughts and
     feelings that run contrary to the fruit of the spirit (e.g., joy, peace,
     patience). What is the prayer of Psalm 51?

8.   Where do we find Psalm 51 within a worship service, and why?

When we practice Confession and Absolution, we confess that we
are all sinners in need of forgiveness. We ourselves break the Eighth
Commandment when we take the things our neighbor says to us in
our pain and share their offenses in the name of "venting" or as a part
of our story. People will always say the wrong thing, but we are in control of how we receive such comments. What is more, we have a God
who tells us to bring it to Him and charge Him with such cares.

Private Confession and Absolution is a wonderful gift from God,
but it isn't practiced as frequently in the Christian community as it
once was. If you have a pastor, it may be helpful to share with him the
ways in which you feel offended and to also ask for forgiveness for
carrying those offenses around instead of forgiving others for them.

PERSONAL REFLECTION

1.   What are some of the hurtful things said to you that you have
     been carrying around with you?

2.   What does being forgiven mean for you? Reflect on the following
     text before answering.

[Know] that you were ransomed from the futile ways inherited
from your forefathers, not with perishable things such as silver
or gold, but with the precious blood of Christ, like that of a lamb
without blemish or spot. (1 Peter 1:18–19)

3. Do you see forgiveness at work in your grieving, and if so, how?

HOMEWORK

As redeemed and beloved children of God, we are called to place the best construction on everything, just as we confess in the Eighth Commandment. That means that even when things are not as we would like them and we receive less-than-helpful comments, we are to assume that rather than meaning to hurt us, our neighbors mean to help. Sometimes putting the best construction on everything can be hard, especially when we are grieving. Most of the time, this is a matter of practice.

I have discovered that when I am faced with various struggles, I gradually become more and more negative. I am a morning person. I can wake up in the morning and sing with the birds and dance with the butterflies, but by nightfall, it is as if a storm cloud hangs over my head. My miscarriage became the rain cloud I woke up under every morning. It forced me to relearn what it means to be joyful and to put the best construction on things. It is easy to take a negative comment and run down into the ground with it while thinking the worst about everything and everyone. If you struggle with the same thing, try practicing rewording the hurtful words of others in a way that places the best construction on them and allows you to more easily forgive others when they say something less than helpful.

You may hear comments like these:

> "At least you know that you can get pregnant."
> "You can have another baby."
> "At least you have other babies."
> "At least you weren't that far along."
> "Maybe it was for the best; the baby probably would have had some kind of disorder or disability."
> "Time heals all wounds."
> "God knows why this happened, and it must have been for the best."
> "God must have needed your baby more."
> "I know what you are going through."
> "God must have known you had your hands full."

For example, if you hear "At least you know that you can get pregnant," you can tell yourself, *I know the person who said this loves me and cares for me because she was trying to comfort me. She doesn't understand that the loss of my child spoils my concern about getting pregnant at this time.*

Or if you hear "God must have needed your baby more" or "God must have known you had your hands full," you can tell yourself, *I know the person who said this loves me and cares for me and he just didn't know what to say in that moment. He might not have been really thinking about what he was saying. I am sorry for this person if he really thinks God takes babies from their mothers because He "needs them more" or because the mother couldn't handle them. This person doesn't have a very good understanding of who God really is and who He shows us to be in His Word.*

Prayer

Heavenly Father, You graciously granted us forgiveness and pardon for all our sins. We thank and praise You for this precious gift that has been given to us through Your Son, Jesus Christ. We ask that You would help us to see Christ in our neighbor, and to remember that we can freely forgive because we have been freely forgiven. Lighten our hearts with the forgiveness that You offer, and help us in times when forgiveness is not felt so easily. We cling to You and the forgiveness that You give in this time of grief. Heal our hearts and make us whole, for the sake of Your Son, Jesus Christ, our Lord. Amen.

Hymn: "Jesus Sinners Doth Receive" (*LSB* 609)

CHAPTER 8

TALKING TO GOD

This chapter will explore how grief can accompany many unexplainable feelings toward God. We will examine biblical ways of expressing those feelings or lack thereof. The topics for study are righteous anger, understanding God's role in the loss of a child, and using the Psalms to understand how to grieve.

VERSE FOR MEDITATION

The LORD is near to the brokenhearted and saves the crushed in spirit.

Psalm 34:18

INTRODUCTION

The first few months of our daughter's life weren't easy for us. She cried a lot, and I knew a pain as a mother that I never knew as a nanny or childcare provider. I recall one of the mothers I worked for telling me, "It physically hurts when I hear my child cry." I told her that it hurt me too, and I thought it did. But I can honestly say now that I had no idea what she was talking about. I held my daughter as she screamed as loudly as her tiny lungs would allow her. Tears rolled down her face, and her mouth was wide open and trembling. She was in pain, and I couldn't do anything about it. I looked at her tiny sad face, and I wanted to cry right along with her.

Why couldn't I do anything? I was torn. Part of me screamed, "Make it stop! Make it stop!" and the other part of me knew those words would do no good; the best I could do was try to remain calm while holding and trying to comfort my one-month-old daughter. So, I held her. I waited helplessly for her pain to subside, continuously reassuring her that I was with her. Those are desperate moments for a new parent who is sleep-deprived and aching for the little life they wanted and waited so long for. Quick fixes and short-term relief are a lifeline in those first months while every sweet and tender moment is fleeting.

In those stressful moments, I often thought on how my own parents did the same with me. They cradled me in their arms and comforted my cries, some of which I can remember from being a bit older. My parents caring for me and caring for my own daughter made me think, *This must be what it is like for God as He holds us in our own distresses.* As we beat upon the chest of God and scream like little babies, "Why? Why? Why?" He remains faithful and holds us while our chins tremble and tears pour forth and we hyperventilate at the death of our children. The one who lost a child becomes the child sobbing in the arms of her Savior, saying, "Please! Make it stop!" He feels the same hurt and pain a mother feels, knowing the best thing for His child is to just remain present while she sobs and her body shakes from grief.

If you want to torture a mother, torture her children and make her watch. So it is for our God, who suffers with us in this sinful, broken world into which He sent His only Son to suffer and die for us. An error I often slip into is thinking there is no way God could know my personal pain. He couldn't possibly know because He doesn't have a uterus and because He never lost a child in the womb or shortly after she was born. While those statements are factual, God does know our pain. God may not have the experience of being a female, but He doesn't need to in order to know our pain. He knows what it is to lose an intimate part of who He is and to watch that part die. God gave of Himself in sacrificing His only Son and allowing Him to die on the cross. He suffered for the death of His Son, and He suffers for the suffering of His children.

In the moments when I suffered most from my miscarriage, I confess that I found little consolation in what I knew to be true of God as a heavenly Father and even less in what He did for me. I wanted to be unique from God and ultimately to feel the pain of grief that came with my loss. I didn't want the cross of Christ to cover my wounds of loss; that seemed far too easy for the complex feelings and problems of pain I faced. Instead, I wanted God to know how much pain I was in, how He really couldn't have any idea what it felt like, and, what is more, that He could have done something to prevent it. I wanted God to know guilt for my pain.

Having moved past that specific pain and desire, I realize that God does know my pain, and I thank Him for not shutting me up in my grief with His righteous anger. After having walked through the darkest days of my grief, I praise Him for being a God who allows us to express anger, frustration, and doubt.

The following reflection is from wife and mother Melissa Jones. She reflects on the comfort of God's Word and the struggle of emotional numbness in the midst of loss.

Praying the Psalms

Shortly after our first son turned one, we found out we were expecting our second child. We were excited to see our family grow and eagerly awaited our first ultrasound appointment. The day arrived, but it wasn't the happy day we thought it would be. We saw our beautiful baby, but his tiny body was completely still. "I'm sorry; there's no heartbeat." We heard the words, but they barely registered. How could our baby have died and I had no idea? We were shocked and devastated, but we trusted the doctors who said that there were probably chromosomal problems and that this kind of loss usually didn't recur. We trusted also in God, who would take care of our precious baby, August. Losing August was the most difficult loss I had faced, but as the days turned into weeks, daily life started to reclaim my attention. My grief receded into the background—still present but not so raw.

After August died, we were desperate to have another baby. Just two months later, we found out we were expecting our third little one. At our first ultrasound at ten weeks, we saw our baby waving around his little arms and legs, his little heart beating so strongly. At fifteen weeks, I felt his first fluttery movements. And then one day, I realized I hadn't felt him in a while. We made an appointment at eighteen weeks to calm my anxiety, but again, we heard those terrible words: "I'm sorry; there's no heartbeat." The next day, I gave birth to our son Owen, so tiny and so perfectly formed.

At first, grieving the death of Owen followed the same pattern as grieving the death of August. After the first month or so, the pain of it lessened. And then the test results started to trickle in. We had decided to pursue tests on Owen and on me to try to determine a cause of death. We prayed for answers, but it was not the will of God that we should have them. Every test came back completely normal.

Since then, grieving has become much more difficult to bear. I cry often over losing Owen; I cry out to God that it isn't fair. Why did he have to die? There was nothing wrong with him, and I wanted to keep him so badly. Why, Lord, did You take him from me?

I can't say that I am mad at God. I don't blame Him for allowing my children to die. I know that my vision is limited and sinful. I can't see where I am going in the future, but I know that God does. And I trust that He is good and will keep His promises. For these reasons, I pray, "Thy will be done." At the same time, I hurt deeply, and my heart is broken. I'm not mad at God; rather, I am sad at God. He is the one on whom I pour out all my "lamentation and bitter weeping" (Jeremiah 31:15). He is the one who hears my endless repetition of "why" questions. Jesus says in Matthew 11:28, "Come to Me, all who labor and are heavy laden, and I will give you rest." To Him I come, heavy laden with sorrow.

When the grief is particularly strong, I feel like Rachel: "A voice is heard in Ramah, lamentation and bitter weeping. Rachel is weeping for her children; she refuses to be comforted for her children, because they are no more" (Jeremiah 31:15). When the sadness is overwhelming and my ears seem deaf to words of comfort, I often look to the Psalms for help. The psalmists put into words what I can only feel:

> How long, O Lord? Will You forget me forever? How long will You hide Your face from me? How long must I take counsel in my soul and have sorrow in my heart all the day? How long shall my enemy be exalted over me?
>
> Consider and answer me, O Lord my God; light up my eyes, lest I sleep the sleep of death, lest my enemy say, "I have prevailed over him," lest my foes rejoice because I am shaken. (Psalm 13:1–4)

Though the context is different, the mood of Psalm 13 mirrors my own, and there is comfort in commiseration. While misery may love company, the Psalms do not allow us to wallow in our sufferings. After David describes the depth of his suffering in Psalm 13, he writes:

> But I have trusted in Your steadfast love; my heart shall rejoice in Your salvation. I will sing to the Lord, because He has dealt bountifully with me. (Psalm 13:5–6)

The sorrow-filled heart rejoices in the Lord; the downcast spirit sings of the Lord's bountiful blessing. In reading Psalm 13 and others like it, I have often pondered how someone can cry and rejoice at the same time. I think it has to do with knowledge versus feeling. I feel the sorrow of Psalm 13:1–4, but I know that God loves me with a steadfast love and has blessed me in so many ways. I just don't feel it right now. My emotions sometimes lead me away into despair, but God brings me back again and again with His Word. His Word reminds me of the life and salvation I have in Christ. His Word paints the picture of a future free from sin, free from death, free from pain. While today may be filled with sorrow, I look to the future with hope, knowing that one day, God will wipe away every tear from my eyes.

Melissa's reflection shows us how words can sometimes fail us. I recall the day that it became obvious that I was going to lose my baby. I had started to bleed, and I felt completely helpless to stop the process in any way. I sobbed and hyperventilated, and I prayed the only thing I could think to pray: "Thy will be done." In my heart, though, I wanted to change the words to "Not Thy will, but *my will* be done!" I wanted a change of circumstances, to be in control, and for my prayer to change God to bend His will to my own. Once I became more rational, my prayer went from saying "Thy will be done" to "I'm sorry. I'm so sorry." I prayed first to God for not trusting Him to care for me amidst the crisis of miscarriage, and I repeatedly said I was sorry to my baby, whom I couldn't save, and to my husband for not being able to carry the life that was made.

I needed words to help me to continue to talk to God, to ask of Him what I knew only He was and is able to offer. I needed help to look to my past and recall the many ways He had cared for His people in their time of trouble and for me in crisis. And I needed help to remember how to cry out to God. His Word is the best place to turn when words fail us. His Word offers the words we can use, sometimes without even realizing it. The Word of God not only offers us comfort in times of distress, but it offers us the very words to say when we can't find them.

THREE THINGS TO FOCUS ON WHEN TALKING TO GOD ABOUT MY LOSS

1. **When feeling angry, look to how God has cared for you in the past and take it up with God, even if the anger is directed at Him.** Had the children of Israel taken their complaints up with God instead of grumbling amongst themselves, the story of the Old Testament might have looked very different. God hears our complaints and asks us to come to Him with all our burdens. When we entrust Him with our anger, we acknowledge our faith in Him as our Lord, who knows our sin and yet loves us still.

2. **When unwilling to accept what has happened, try to continue to pray as He taught us: "Your will be done."** Even when we don't like what is happening and we don't want to accept it, praying as He taught us can help us move through the grief because His words can be the easiest to turn to, to recall, and to focus on when nothing seems to make sense.

3. **When at a loss for words, pray the Psalms.** As was shown in our reflection, the Psalms help us to have focus and direction in our grieving. They often have the words that we are having difficulty expressing. And they show us that we are not alone in our sentiments of feeling alone, frustrated, abandoned, and unheard by God.

Scripture Discussion and Reflection

History is an amazing thing! It shows us where we have been, and it can sometimes tell us where we are going should history repeat itself. We can look back and often clearly identify times when God's strong hand was guiding us. In the midst of the storm, however, we may be told to focus more on the moment and less on the past. Sometimes we are only trying to survive. When we are in survival mode, we may be weary, worn, depressed, and altogether hopeless. While trying to sustain faith with the Word of God and learning to live with grief at the same time, it is important to look to your past and recall how God has brought His people through past times of grief.

Take a look at the following verses and consider the history of not only the children of Israel and the promises God made to them, but also the history of all mankind:

> You shall serve the LORD your God, and He will bless your bread and your water, and I will take sickness away from among you. None shall miscarry or be barren in your land; I will fulfill the number of your days. (Exodus 23:25–26)

> You shall be blessed above all peoples. There shall not be male or female barren among you or among your livestock. (Deuteronomy 7:14)

These texts from Exodus and Deuteronomy show us something interesting about the history of God with His people and about miscarriage and being barren. It shows us how God acknowledges the span and depth to which these two things affect a people. He counts it as blessing to take this problem away from the people. It gives new meaning to Genesis 3:16, where we read:

> To the woman He said, "I will surely multiply your pain in childbearing; in pain you shall bring forth children. Your desire shall be contrary to your husband, but he shall rule over you."

The pain God talks about is not just the physical aspect of pushing a child into the world; it is everything that surrounds the hours of labor and delivery. It's the suffering that comes in nights of worrying if your baby is okay. It also includes silenced echoes and stilled sonograms with broken hearts on the other end of them. Pain in childbearing includes empty cribs and rockers that are retired too soon. Pain in childbearing has to do with miscarriage, stillbirth, infant loss, and being barren. All are the result of sin.

1. Read Genesis 3:9–15 in your Bible. In recalling our history, why is it important to include and understand Genesis 3 as our story as well?

2. Whom does the man blame for his falling into temptation, and what is the order and manner of God's response?

3. When grieving the loss of a child, why does it become important to place everything upon God, even if it is blame?

We can see in the account of the fall into sin how fear, grief, and shame consumed man so that he no longer knew how to converse with God. Even when man talked to God with such a lack of respect, God conveyed His plan in Genesis 3:15 to restore the relationship between the two of them. Take a look at Luke 22:41–43:

> And He withdrew from them about a stone's throw, and knelt down and prayed, saying, "Father, if You are willing, remove this cup from Me. Nevertheless, not My will, but Yours, be done." And there appeared to Him an angel from heaven, strengthening Him.

4. In Genesis 3:15, we see the very first proclamation of a Savior, and in Luke 22:42 we see Christ praying to His Father as the offspring of woman who would bruise the head of Satan. How is Genesis 3:15 the answer to Christ's prayer seen in Luke 22:42? What was the will of the Father?

5. Why is Christ's prayer a necessary one, even when He knew what the will of the Father was?

6.   Where and when are Christ's words "not My will, but Yours, be done" made our own?

Just as the words and example of Christ serve us in our grieving and communicating with God, so does the Bible as a whole. Again, one book of the Bible that can help us converse with and express anger with God is the Book of Psalms. The Psalms help us in expressing anger with God because

- They are songs, laments, and prayers addressed to God that hold God as the focal point. (This means that they also acknowledge God to be God, even in the midst of anger and crisis.)

- They offer structure and ways to lament life and question God when grief leaves us speechless.

- They return praises to God and recognize the good He has done in the past and will continue to do for the future.

Read Psalm 88 and consider how it fits the three ways addressed above that show how the Psalms help us in expressing anger with God. Write your thoughts here.

7.   What are some of the complaints the psalmist places before God? More specifically, for what particular things does the psalmist blame God?

8.   Out of 150 psalms, Psalm 88 is the only one that does not return praise back to God. What hints does this psalm provide as to why the psalmist does not return praise, and why is this significant for someone who is grieving?

PERSONAL REFLECTION

1.   Can you identify specific times in your life when you have had a difficult time talking to God or praising Him as a direct result of your grief and loss?

2. Can you recall an event from your history that shows you that God has been present and caring for you in the midst of grief?

3. What does praying "not my will, but Yours, be done" mean for you in the midst of your grieving?

HOMEWORK

Take some time to skim through the Psalms. Try to find one that speaks about what it is that you are struggling with most as a result of your loss. Write out the psalm in a journal, or write out the specific verses you identify with, and expand on them as if you were using them to start a prayer. Throughout the week, take time to revisit the psalm you selected, read it, and rewrite it. At the end of seven days, consider how you may have used the psalm to express many different things to God throughout the week.

PRAYER

Gracious heavenly Father, You have brought us through many storms in our lives and spared us from many trials and difficulties. Draw near to us even when we push against You and question why You have allowed us to suffer grief. Keep us mindful of You and dependent upon Your grace and mercy. Teach us to desire Your will when our only desire is for ourselves and our lost children. For the sake of Your Son, Jesus Christ. Amen.

HYMN: "JESUS, LEAD THOU ON" (*LSB* 718)

CHAPTER 9

I BELIEVE, HELP MY UNBELIEF

Our final chapter will explore some of the difficult questions that are answered by trusting God and what He tells us in His Word, not by listening to the ever-rising questions, Satan's whispers, that cause us to doubt His goodness toward us. This study will seek to lay a foundation of truths that a mother can go to when seeds of doubt begin to rob her of the comfort that has been promised to her.

VERSE FOR MEDITATION

For You formed my inward parts; You knitted me together in my mother's womb. I praise You, for I am fearfully and wonderfully made. Wonderful are Your works; my soul knows it very well.

Psalm 139:13–14

INTRODUCTION

Miscarriage will shake your faith and rock your foundations to the core, sometimes violently and other times subtly. It can cause a woman to doubt and question fundamental beliefs and cling to false hopes. When working through grief, it is especially challenging when false hope is revealed as just that—false hope. In our broken state, we want to cling to and believe any hopeful and promising news we are given. When we have learned to cling to a promise or a word of hope that turns out to be false, we push against what is true and we defend our false hopes, rejecting our fundamental beliefs. Our sure foundation is Christ. He is all we need to know and to cling to in times of grief. He is the way and the truth and the life (John 14:6). He never forsakes us.

For this reason, anything that does not proclaim this sure and certain confession is false hope. False hopes can cause us to doubt because they create for us a faith that is separate from and outside of what is promised to us in God's Word. We must always challenge ourselves in the things we *want* to hear so that we do not become comfortable believing something that is not true to who God tells us He is.

I never doubted my faith in God while in the midst of grieving; I simply just believed. For me, to doubt faith in God would be to deny Him, and I didn't have the strength to do that. It was much easier to just believe as a child believes in God. My simple belief, however, was deeply seeded with other doubts that were indirectly connected to God. Satan doesn't have to work too hard on a person who has lost a child because her doubts alone can carry her to places too dark to give utterance to in the day. Grieving my children who died in the womb came in phases, and each day brought a different set of doubts. At first, I doubted whether I was allowed to grieve them, since I had not had sufficient time to bond with them. Later, I doubted my sanity and thought perhaps I was being hysterical since my own husband didn't seem to be grieving the same way I was. I doubted if God really valued and saved the short-lived life in my womb; after all, my babies never made it to the baptismal font. I doubted God's goodness in answering prayers for children, and I doubted His wisdom for allowing things to happen in the way they did. I never doubted, though, that I had salvation; I never doubted Christ's saving work on the cross. But I doubted so many other things that filtered into what I knew about God.

It would have been easy for me to take what I knew and create what I wanted to think and believe in the midst of my miscarriage. It might have even felt "faith affirming" to accept little platitudes like "Jesus is caring for my babies until I can get to heaven to take over." After reflecting on the many popular comforts that follow miscarriage, I realized that they don't just say something about my doubts; they say something about the kind of image I make God into. What kind of a God and heaven do we believe in if we need to believe that there is a nursery there where Jesus sits, not at the right hand of God but in a rocking chair, nursing all the little lost babies? As Christians, we need our God, specifically God the Son, to be much bigger than that. We need the God that we confess in the Creed, the one who overcame death and therefore proclaims victory over sin, death, and the devil. We need Christ to be *God* for us and for our babies, not a nanny. Infants are so fragile, and any mother will tell you that she sneaks into the baby's bedroom in the middle of the night just to make sure her baby is still breathing. What kind of heaven would we be believing in if our babies still needed that kind of care?

It is a frightening thing to entrust the life of one you love into the hands of another. I recall my first night home with my daughter. Until we were able to buy her a crib, my husband wanted to hold and keep her in the bed with us. I was terrified all night that my husband would roll over and crush her or forget that she was in bed with us. I woke him up periodically to check and make sure he remembered that he was holding our daughter. One would think that it is much easier to entrust small lives to our heavenly Father, but in reality, we are much like I was that first night home with my newborn daughter and husband. We doubt God can care for our children as we would. In our mind, we want salvation for our children, but we want them to know that salvation in their old age. We want to believe that God will work miracles for our children. And we want to remain doubtful that He would allow us to pass through dark days in burying them.

Faith in God is woven intricately into our understanding of who Christ is. Christ is God, and we need to understand that false hopes begin when we try to make Christ into what we want Him to be. Our belief in Christ must be founded on the deeper meaning of His death and resurrection in order to help our unbelief. Believing in Christ and His cross doesn't mean that we are immune to suffering; rather, we should expect suffering in this sin-sick world. But in that suffering, we can also expect Christ to be present all the more clearly.

The following reflection is from Stephanie Traphagan, a pastor's wife and mother to three. She reflects on what doubts she struggled with most in facing her miscarriage and how her confession, Scripture, and prayer helped in the midst of those doubts.

"Jeremiah Is with Jesus"

The bleeding started ten minutes before church. Barely enough time to get my children into shoes and out the door. Certainly not enough time to tell my pastor husband, especially just minutes before church. I don't remember anything from the service. It was all I could do to wrangle Sarah and Timothy and choke back the panic and tears that threatened to erupt. *Lord, have mercy! My baby.*

It didn't stop. All Sunday, I told myself there was still hope, that this wasn't for sure, plenty of women had some bleeding in pregnancy. Monday morning, minutes ticked as I waited to call the midwife. Bloodwork, she said, was the first step. Bill took me, and we spent hours in an agonizing wait for the results. In the end, they were inconclusive. I'd have to do another draw in two days. We drove home, and while Bill tried to stay positive, my hope was fizzling. We sat together on the couch and sang hymns.

> In God, my faithful God,
> I trust when dark my road;
> Great woes may overtake me,
> Yet He will not forsake me.
> My troubles He can alter;
> His hand lets nothing falter.

(*LSB* 745:1)

The road was certainly looking dark.

By that night, the bleeding had increased enough that the midwives suggested it was time for the ER. We packed up the kids in their jammies and told our friends we'd be dropping them at their house on the way to the hospital. The last time we'd made a middle-of-the-night appearance like this was just hours before Timothy was born. This time, it was hours before our worst nightmare.

Sarah came out to the car as Bill and Luke took the babies inside. She opened the driver's door and leaned in. "It's not looking good," I choked out.

"Oh, Steph." She climbed in to hug me and look me in the eyes. "You are a baptized child of God. Jesus loves you and your baby." I have clung to those simple words and their simple truth and wisdom.

Our time at the hospital was awful. We were left alone, abandoned to our greatest fears over and over, exhausted in the cold, sterile room. Finally, the doctor came in and confirmed what I was already sure he would say: I was in the middle of a miscarriage. He had nothing better to say to me than that nature knew what it was doing with these things, and I'd probably be bleeding a lot and pass some "tissue," as medical experts so euphemize small babies.

We left the ER in a haze, angry at all the hospital staff who kept wishing us a better night. Minutes before returning to our friends' house, I convulsed over in pain and nausea, telling Bill I was about to be sick. It was well after midnight, and we crept into their house, then I ran to the bathroom. Just a few minutes later, I knew it was over. I had delivered our baby, dead, in their toilet.

None of us knew what to do. Sarah and Luke had awoken by then, and it was they who rescued him from the toilet. His tiny body in a plastic tub, they tried to hide the sight from me, but I insisted on seeing. My baby. They filled a cooler with ice. There was nothing left to do but sleep.

In the morning, Luke cooked eggs and made coffee. We sat at their table with the children and talked about anything except what had happened. Like my high school world history class, for whatever reason. In time, they kept our kids and sent us home to rest.

We'd hardly rounded the corner when I said to Bill, in a tiny voice, "Can we give him a name?" Yes. And the first name to both of our minds was the same—Lazarus. The one Jesus raised from the dead. Later that day, after a few hours of sleep, I cocooned myself in the corner of the couch and compiled a list of possible names. His name had to mean something. It had to confess what we believed about this baby. In the end, it was an easy decision. Jeremiah—"the Lord has uplifted," and the one commemorated on that awful day of waiting and praying. Lazarus—"my God has helped." I never doubted our baby's salvation. The Lord is able to help and uplift unborn babies just as He can all sinful beings. "Jeremiah is with Jesus," we repeated to our other children, raised from death just like his namesake.

His committal was that Friday. We buried Jeremiah in the church cemetery fifteen minutes from our house, last in line of the children's row. Timothy's godfather came and spoke God's Word to us, and we were surrounded by friends and their children as we sang hymns and filled our ears with Christ's promises.

> Lord, let at last Thine angels come,
> To Abr'ham's bosom bear me home,
> That I may die unfearing;
> And in its narrow chamber keep
> My body safe in peaceful sleep
> Until Thy reappearing.
> And then from death awaken me,
> That these mine eyes with joy may see,
> O Son of God, Thy glorious face,
> My Savior and my fount of grace.
> Lord Jesus Christ, my prayer attend, my prayer attend,
> And I will praise Thee without end.
>
> (*LSB* 708:3)

Leaving Jeremiah's tiny casket in the ground is one of the hardest things I have ever done, but we did not leave him without hope.

One week later, I attended the funeral for another baby, stillborn at twenty-three weeks. Attending another funeral so soon, for another baby, was almost too much to bear, but I knew I should be there. And the words of the hymns and sermon spoke straight to my heart. Again, the pastor preached of Christ's promises and how even in the womb these children hear the Word and can receive the gift of faith. God hears the prayer of Christian parents on behalf of their children.

We continue to cling tightly to God's promises, and I do not doubt that our baby is with Jesus. Jeremiah Lazarus's own grave marker confesses where our hope lies, stating, "Jesus crucified for me." This was Bill's suggestion, from *LSB* 422:

> On my heart imprint Your image,
> Blessed Jesus, King of grace,
> That life's riches, cares, and pleasures
> Never may Your work erase;
> Let the clear inscription be:
> Jesus, crucified for me,
> Is my life, my hope's foundation,
> And my glory and salvation!

We couldn't think of anything more perfect and succinct. The clear inscription, indeed. Here lies our hope.

In addition to the many hymns we turned to for comfort in those first difficult days, I found my own head swirling with words. Less than two weeks after we lost Jeremiah, I sat with a notebook in a camp chair while Sarah and Timothy played in the yard. The words overflowed.

In Blood

> Brought forth in blood to gruesome death
> Dark, cold, alone, no sight, no breath
> My fallen one, the womb your grave
> Hear Rachel's cry still echoing
>
> Laid down in blood, entombed in earth
>
> No count of days—your death: your birth
> From dust to dust now these remains
> Await in sleep the Day of Grace
>
> Raised up in blood, exalted one

His death, your life, your hope, your crown
New life delivered from the cross
One day to rise like Lazarus

Robed white in blood before the throne
No longer mine but made Christ's own
Alive this fallen one now stands
With angels and the sainted band

I know that Jeremiah is with the Lord. I have never doubted that. But that doesn't mean I haven't been plagued with doubt amidst my grief. It simply wore a different mask.

The truth is, my reaction to our third pregnancy was ambivalent at best. While we certainly believe that every baby is a gift from God, and I knew I would eventually grow into excitement, I was not exactly planning for another blessing at that particular moment. With two toddlers already, I was feeling the full weight of motherhood, and it was hard. So very hard. I wasn't sure how I was going to make it with another baby. So it was with mixed feelings that I told family and friends we were expecting again, and only after giving myself some time to get used to the idea.

Then, just a few short weeks later, we lost him.

Dark voices were already whispering in my mind, but one comment I received as we announced the miscarriage haunted me. Amid the "so sorrys," one person, attempting to be helpful (and utterly failing), said, "God must have known you already had your hands full," with a knowing glance at Sarah and Timothy. I don't think I actually said anything in response, but my heart clenched.

What if? What if that person was right? What if I had wanted the baby more? What if I was a better, more capable mother—someone who yelled less, disciplined more fairly? Maybe then . . . maybe I wouldn't have lost him. These doubts were so dark and ugly that I told no one, not even my husband. And in my numerous journal entries of that time, I never once gave them voice. They were simply too terrible. I did my best to push them aside, but I couldn't silence them completely.

About six weeks after the miscarriage, Bill and I were attending Doxology, a retreat for pastors and their wives. It was a welcome respite from the trials we'd been facing, and I had been looking forward to attending church and actually being able to listen. Private confession was offered that morning before the service, but we didn't arrive in time. Nonetheless, I found myself thinking about what I would have said if we had. And I broke down, because the answer was obvious. I would have confessed the miscarriage. I sobbed through the entire service. My teeth chattered and my body shook as the guilt and grief and what-ifs of Jeremiah's death overtook me.

After the Benediction, as the other couples trickled out to sectional speakers, I spluttered to Bill, "I need a pastor." A few minutes later, trembling, I sat before one and confessed all my dark, ugly doubts, how I hadn't really wanted to be pregnant, and what if that person was right and my hands were already too full? I didn't know how I was going to do it with another baby, and then he died. What if, somehow, it had been my fault?

This pastor took me by the hand and told me these were lies from the devil. The wages of sin is death, and even in the womb, our Jeremiah had a sinful nature. But God does not punish His children by taking our babies' lives. No amount of my excitement or adequacy in motherhood could have saved my baby. But thanks be to God—Jesus' death on the cross can and has. This pastor continued to speak words of God's forgiveness and comfort to me, and after a time, I was able to rise, wipe my eyes, and go, sad, but my heart stilled.

While I can't say these doubts never rise anymore, I am much more able to see them as the devil's accusations and silence them in the name of Jesus. It is the Lord who gives, and while we do not know why He has taken Jeremiah away, we do know we will see him again. Blessed be the name of the Lord.

There are so many questions that are raised when you lose a child. At the core of our questioning is doubt. We may feel and think that we are completely trusting in God, but in our own finite wisdom, we would always say that it would have been better if our children were still alive. We doubt if God really had our best interests at heart when He allowed for our children to be taken from us. We might wonder with Stephanie, did God have a specific reason that I don't know about for allowing my child to die before entering the world? We also wonder what happens to children who die before they are baptized. These are difficult doubts because they question God in His mercy and what is not clearly defined in the Bible. We cannot stray from what God says in His Word to understand better why He has allowed us to suffer as His servant Job did. We don't get to paint God as we want to see Him to make our personal struggles with grief easier. Believing in a God who takes away with the same hand that He uses to give becomes a struggle of doubt. Does God really care? Is God really merciful? Did God really *allow* this to happen?

What Is Needful in the Midst of Doubts

1. **Clinging to a confession and what is known.** In the midst of doubt, we have been given a great foundation to hold onto by remembering what we believe and confess about God as the Creator, Redeemer, and Sanctifier.

2. **Scripture.** While the Word of God does not give direct answers for the loss of a child, there are still comforting promises to be found.

3. **Prayer.** Through the gift of prayer, we are invited to *cast our children upon God* and to pray for their spiritual life more than their physical life.

Scripture Discussion and Reflection

What we know: every Sunday is an opportunity to make confession of our faith in the fellowship of all believers. How often do we take time to review and reflect on the "What does this mean?" that we read in the Small Catechism? When we confess the Apostles' Creed, we are saying in brief what we believe. Let's take a look at the three parts of the Creed with explanations as they apply to us in our doubts. (Refer to "Explanation of the Apostles' Creed" beginning on p. 167.)

> For You formed my inward parts; You knitted me together in my mother's womb. I praise You, for I am fearfully and wonderfully made. Wonderful are Your works; my soul knows it very well. (Psalm 139:13–14)

1. Psalm 139 and the First Article with explanation confess God as Creator. What is the significance of believing and confessing God to be Creator over all when we take into consideration having lost a child?

Sometimes when faced with loss, we try to create a different God that sits well with us, and we try to explain things that just don't make sense, not because of God but because we live in a broken sinful world. I recall a girl I met when I was in middle school. She was at church events and in dance classes with me. She was an ambitious, beautiful, well-liked girl, and it happened that she was killed in a car accident. I recall the dance instructors distributing sheets of paper to us all with the words "In Memory of" and a poem that attempted to add beauty and meaning for God's reasoning in allowing her to be killed. The poem talked about how God was like a gardener and this particular girl was like a flower and how sometimes God goes out to His garden and wants some of the pretty flowers for Himself to make all those "ugly old flowers" seem a bit more beautiful. Something in that poem seemed off to me, even at my young age, and just not right. I kept thinking, "That isn't how God is."

Read the last few lines of the explanation of the First Article of the Apostles' Creed:

> All this He does only out of fatherly, divine goodness and mercy, without any merit or worthiness in me. For all this it is my duty to thank and praise, serve and obey Him. This is most certainly true.

Now take a look at Deuteronomy 32:39, where God says:

> See now that I, even I, am He, and there is no god beside Me; I kill and I make alive; I wound and I heal; and there is none that can deliver out of My hand.

2. How might this confession and Bible verse go against thoughts among women who share the common experience of having lost a child, but not a common confession? Think of some of the typical platitudes or words of "comfort" used in circles of those who have lost children. Can you identify how this confession and the verse from Deuteronomy can be comforting when compared with the false hope that we have been clinging to?

Sometimes the idea of God taking a child before he or she can be baptized is more challenging to understand than when the opportunity is given to baptize the child. Baptism is a hope and promise to cling to when a child is lost, but what about those who don't even get the opportunity to baptize their child before he or she dies? The Psalms talk about being "cast upon God" from birth, and God being the God of the unborn. Take a look at Psalm 22:9–10:

> Yet You are He who took me from the womb; You made me trust You at my mother's breasts. On You was I cast from my birth, and from my mother's womb You have been my God.

3. What comfort can these verses offer to parents who weren't able to baptize their child, and how is the understanding of God as Creator, who also makes alive and kills, a form of Gospel for someone struggling with the same loss?

4. In the Second Article of the Apostles' Creed, we confess Christ
    as Redeemer. If we were to break down the Second Article with
    its explanation into four parts—He came, He died, He rose, and
    He will come again—what would be the key points for someone
    dealing with the loss of a child to apply to their situation when
    reflecting on each part?

He came:

He died:

He rose:

He will come again:

5. In the Third Article of the Creed, we find the sum of all that is
    hoped for by those whose faith is in Christ: "the resurrection of
    the body, and the life everlasting. Amen." What significance does
    this have in light of the loss of a child and the grief that accompa-
    nies that loss?

Having a strong foundation for who you believe and confess God
to be helps to confront false hopes that could otherwise misguide you
into thinking things that aren't supported by your foundational belief
and confession. The other base on which we must always be building
our knowledge and to which we must go for reference is the very Word
of God. As stated before, the Bible has little to say on the specific topic
of miscarriage and infant loss, but that does not mean it is completely
silent. Let's take a look at the following texts.

> But God shows His love for us in that while we were still sinners,
> Christ died for us. (Romans 5:8)

> For God did not send His Son into the world to condemn the
> world, but in order that the world might be saved through
> Him. Whoever believes in Him is not condemned, but whoever
> does not believe is condemned already, because he has not be-

lieved in the name of the only Son of God. (John 3:17–18)

And He said to them, "Go into all the world and proclaim the gospel to the whole creation. Whoever believes and is baptized will be saved, but whoever does not believe will be condemned." (Mark 16:15–16)

So faith comes from hearing, and hearing through the word of Christ. (Romans 10:17)

Let me ask you only this: Did you receive the Spirit by works of the law or by hearing with faith? Are you so foolish? Having begun by the Spirit, are you now being perfected by the flesh? Did you suffer so many things in vain—if indeed it was in vain? Does He who supplies the Spirit to you and works miracles among you do so by works of the law, or by hearing with faith? (Galatians 3:2–5)

And she [Mary] entered the house of Zechariah and greeted Elizabeth. And when Elizabeth heard the greeting of Mary, the baby leaped in her womb. And Elizabeth was filled with the Holy Spirit, and she exclaimed with a loud cry, "Blessed are you among women, and blessed is the fruit of your womb!" (Luke 1:40–42)

6. The texts above follow a train of thought that is intended to lead us to make an educated understanding, based on biblical texts, about an infant who dies without being baptized. Answer the questions below to follow this train of thought.

    What does Romans say about *when* Christ died for us?

    What do John and Mark identify as being that which saves   and that which condemns? (Stick to the text and use only the words from the text.)

    Where does faith come from, based on Romans 10:17?

Who carries out or sustains our faith as shown in Galatians 3:2–5?

What caused the baby to leap within the womb as seen in Luke 1:40–42?

7. What conclusions can be drawn from each of these texts as they relate to infants within the womb?

The Bible provides few examples where someone has lost a child, and there isn't anything that talks about the loss of a child as it relates to Baptism. What we do have is the example of King David, which also can be comforting to recall and reflect on.

Read 2 Samuel 12:16–23 in your Bible and look for David's response during the life of his child and after the life of his child. Also identify on what day the child died and why this is significant when considering children who die in the womb before they have the chance to be baptized.

There are a few things implied in the text that aren't explicitly spelled out. This may be due to the fact that it was documented by a culture that would have understood what was being said without spelling out the various aspects of grief and promise found in the text. The first thing to take note of is the day on which the child died. The text is very specific to point out, "On the seventh day the child died" (v. 18). Take a look at Genesis 17:10–14 and identify why this would have been of great significance for David and the Jewish culture.

> [God said,] "This is My covenant, which you shall keep, between Me and you and your offspring after you: Every male among you shall be circumcised. You shall be circumcised in the flesh of your foreskins, and it shall be a sign of the covenant between Me and you. He who is eight days old among you shall be circumcised. Every male throughout your generations, whether born in your house or bought with your money from any foreigner who is not of your offspring, both he who is born in your house and he who is bought with your money, shall surely be circumcised. So shall

My covenant be in your flesh an everlasting covenant. Any uncircumcised male who is not circumcised in the flesh of his foreskin
shall be cut off from his people; he has broken My covenant."
(Genesis 17:10–14)

8. Based on this text, what would have been especially disconcerting
for David in the fact that his son died on the seventh day?

The second thing to take note of is David's response to his servants.
His servants expected greater mourning at the death of the child than
during the life of the child, and David's response goes against what
they thought was appropriate:

While the child was still alive, I fasted and wept, for I said, "Who
knows whether the Lord will be gracious to me, that the child
may live?" But now he is dead. Why should I fast? Can I bring
him back again? I shall go to him, but he will not return to me.
(2 Samuel 12:22–23)

9. What does David's response tell us about his understanding of
grief and of where his hope was in time of grieving?

If you lost a child before given the chance to baptize him or her,
you may have received two different responses from clergy as to God's
handling of your child. The preferred response is always "Your child
is in heaven." And the less-than-preferred response is "I can't say for
sure where your child is because Scripture doesn't give a clear definition of what happens to children who aren't baptized." Essentially, the
second response says, "I want to tell you your child is in heaven, but I
can't stray from what I know is in Scripture." For the grieving parent,
this produces a doubt that questions God's goodness without knowing
how to recall His goodness. While this response may seem cold and
lacking compared with what we want to hear when we are suffering the
physical death of a child, the better way of saying the same thing is to
proclaim what we do know. That is, we know, like David, that God is
merciful and He hears our prayers.

Dr. Martin Luther writes, "Because the mother is a believing Christian it is to be hoped that her heartfelt cry and deep longing to bring her child to be baptized will be accepted by God as an effective prayer."[8] And sixteenth-century theologian Martin Chemnitz wrote:

> Are, then, the children of believers who die before birth or in birth damned? By no means, but since our children, brought to the light by divine blessing, are, as it were, given into our hands and at the same time means are offered, or it is made possible for the seal of the covenant of grace to be applied to them, there indeed that very solemn divine statement applies: The man-child, the flesh of whose foreskin is not circumcised on the eighth day, his soul shall be blotted out from [his] people (Gn 17:14). Hence the Lord met Moses on the way and wanted to kill him, because he had neglected to circumcise [his] son (Ex 4:24–26). But when those means are not given us—as when in the Old Testament a male died before the eighth day of circumcision—likewise when they, who, born in the desert in the interval of 40 years, could not be circumcised because of daily harassment by enemies and constant wanderings, died uncircumcised, Jos 5:5–6, and when today infants die before they are born—in such cases the grace of God is not bound to the Sacraments, but those infants are to be brought and commended to Christ in prayers. And one should not doubt that those prayers are heard, for they are made in the name of Christ. Jn 16:23; Gn 17:7; Mt 19:14. Since, then, we cannot bring infants as yet unborn to Christ through Baptism, therefore we should do it through pious prayers. Parents are to be put in mind of this, and if perhaps such a case occur, they are to be encouraged with this comfort.[9]

Neither theologian says anything about the grieving parent knowing where a child finds his or her rest, but rather trusting in God to be merciful, to be a God who answers the earnest prayers of His people. It should come as a great comfort to know that the fate of our children

---

8   AE 43:247–48.
9   Chemnitz, *Ministry, Word, and Sacraments*, 119–20.

does not rest in our actions but in the mercy of God, who is not as limited as we sometimes make Him out to be.

One thing David was certain of was that he could "go to" his son, and what gave him this certainty? In 2 Samuel 12:14, we see Nathan the prophet telling David that the consequences of his sin would be death. David knew God had given the word for his son to die, but it did not stop David from praying on behalf of his child. In addition, after his child's death, he goes to the house of the Lord to worship. This is not to say he was not grieving, but rather he was incorporating God into his grief with a knowledge and understanding of who he confessed God to be. We do not know exactly what David prayed for, only that he prayed on behalf of the child. He could have been praying that God would grant days, months, or years to the child's earthly life, or he could have been praying that God would receive the child into His kingdom. The point is that he directed his petitions and conversation toward God for as long as the child was with him.

The greatest lesson we can learn from David, as parents of children who have been entrusted to the care of the Lord, is to pray for our children while they are with us and trust in what we know to be true of God. We know we live in a broken world that is full of sin, and we know the result of sin is death. This knowledge should bring us to our knees all the more. After losing my first to miscarriage, I lived in fear of losing every child. That first death busted open my life to the reality that no one is immune to the effects of sin, that there is no promise that life will be seamlessly brought into this world, and that some beginnings end before they have a good start. I had to learn to silence my fear by praying to God that no matter what happened, He would give my children a spiritual life before a physical one. I prayed also for myself, that I would honestly desire that my children know the Lord before they knew my face. It is not an easy prayer for a parent longing to hold her child in her arms, but the arms of our God are much stronger—strong enough to be extended upon a cross to suffer and die not just for my sins but the sins of all mankind.

Personal Reflection

1. What are some ideas or beliefs that bring you comfort in the loss of your child?

2. How do those ideas support what God tells us in His Word?

3. What is the most comforting promise in God's Word that you have found to cling to while you have been grieving?

Homework

Often our prayer life can be lacking, and we fail to recognize how God shows Himself to be faithful to us through answering prayers. The problem is that we often just say prayers in passing or in the moment of need and we never revisit and see how our prayers were answered. We may even disregard prayer as being worthless or only for asking things of God, when prayer can also be for simply conversing with a good and gracious God.

Try starting a discipline of keeping a prayer journal. Perhaps you can start by just writing out names, subjects, and worries in bulleted form in the study portions of this book. Try to work up to committing to the same writing but in a blank book. Over time, perhaps your writings will become more detailed. When you have been writing over a period of time, you will be able to look back at what you wrote to pray about and see how God has answered your prayers in various ways. The act of writing out your prayers will help you give attention to the gift of communication with God in a way that will also help remind you that God does not take our prayers lightly, even though we might not see Him answering in ways we would like.

Prayer

Gracious heavenly Father, You calm our doubts by being our anchor to cling to and confess in times of grief and loss. Be with us no matter what doubts consume us and shake us. Keep us firm in You and always looking not only to the saving work of Your Son on the cross but also to You as our Creator and the Sustainer of our faith. Bless us and keep us steadfast in Your Word, through Jesus Christ, Your Son, our Lord. Amen.

HYMN: "IN GOD, MY FAITHFUL GOD" (*LSB* 745)

CONTRIBUTING MOTHERS

Reflection 1: Kristina Odom is the wife of a pastor and a mother of seven children. Of them, she gets to care for three here on earth, grow one in her womb, and wait and long for three in heaven. Before getting married, she lived her life in a faraway country, growing up in a large, loving family, working as a registered nurse for many years, and studying theology. It was during these studies that she met her husband and moved to the United States.

Reflection 2: Melissa DeGroot is a deaconess in the LCMS, wife to a wonderful pastor, mother to one goofy and bright almost-seven-year-old son, and friend to many. She has contributed to other works on the topic of barrenness and miscarriage through the book *He Remembers the Barren* and a blog of the same name. She enjoys spending time with her family, homeschooling her son, cooking, and exercising.

Reflection 3: Rebecca Kearney is a Christian, daughter, wife, mom, and friend. She lives in Southern California with her husband, Arlie. They have been married for nearly ten years after meeting on a mission trip to build a playground in Vietnam. Rebecca is a former high school English teacher who is currently on a mommy sabbatical with her three daughters, Quinn, Emma, and Kate. It was the birth and loss of their second daughter, Hannah Grace, that propelled Rebecca to become a stay-at-home mom and writer, although she has always loved the significance and importance of words. It is her sincere hope that their family's story of infant loss is one that brightens the dark despair that accompanies such grief and brings the hope of Jesus to those who know these same depths of loss and sorrow.

Reflection 4: Kendra Voss is a deaconess student at Concordia Theological Seminary in Fort Wayne, Indiana. She loves country life in Homestead, Iowa, with her husband, who is a pastor. She enjoys the time she spends with the ladies of LWML, photography, and cooking and preserving food, as well as showing hospitality to friends and family alike. Kendra enjoys her vocation as wife and is adjusting to her vocation as mother to two babies, Elisha Solomon and Ruth Abigail, who are in heaven. Elisha Solomon knew his parents' love for nine short weeks, from July to September of 2016. Ruth Abigail Voss was entrusted into Christ's care on July 3, 2017, when she was born still at twenty-three weeks. During her twenty-three weeks of life inside the womb, Ruth heard sixty-nine Old Testament lessons, sixty-nine Epistle lessons, and sixty-nine Gospel lessons, not to mention the twenty-three sermons and countless hymns. Kendra is thankful for the pastors who showed her how much her daughter had already heard the Word even before she was born. It gives her comfort knowing that faith comes from hearing the Word and that Ruth Abigail and Elisha Solomon both heard the Word daily. Ruth was prayed for by people literally all over the world. Her little life had an impact on so many people. It's because of that that Kendra wishes to encourage the faith of those who suffer miscarriage and infant loss and to speak on behalf of all the babies who cannot speak for themselves.

Reflection 5: Kristen Gregory was born and raised in Iowa, and she came to the Church in high school through some dear neighbors. She attended college in Hillsdale, Michigan, where she met her husband, Pastor Peter Gregory. She loves fiction, reading aloud, gardening, knitting, and spending time with friends. She is a homeschool mom of four in Westminster, Massachusetts. Peter and Kristen are, the Lord willing, expecting another child in June 2018.

Reflection 6: Audrey Daenzer is a pastor's wife in rural North Dakota and a stay-at-home mom. She holds degrees in music and library science, but she always hoped to become a wife and mother. She and her husband have two little girls and are expecting their fourth child in the spring. Their third daughter, Perpetua, is with her Lord after dying in the womb at seventeen weeks. Audrey loves solid Lutheran hymns, the smell of old books, new and adventurous recipes, the first crocuses of spring, and a good plate of sushi. She looks for "the resurrection of the dead and the life of the world to come."

Reflection 7: Kathryn Ziegler Weber is first and foremost a baptized child of God. She is wife to pastor, husband, and father Roberto Alejandro Weber. She had two miscarriages before giving birth to a beautiful daughter named Evangelina Lucía. She lives in Miramar, Argentina, where she supports and serves unofficially as a deaconess to the two congregations where her husband serves as a pastor. She studied at Concordia University Nebraska, where she received her BA in psychology, and at Concordia Theological Seminary, Fort Wayne, Indiana, where she received her MA in theological studies. She was commissioned as an LCMS deaconess in 2015 at First Lutheran Church in Papillion, Nebraska. Kathryn served as a missionary and deaconess to the Dominican Republic for three years before marrying and moving to Argentina. She enjoys contemplating the gift of her Baptism and serving the Lord with a joyful heart, and she also enjoys nap time with her daughter.

Reflection 8: Melissa Jones earned a master of arts in deaconess studies from Concordia Seminary, St. Louis, in 2014. At the same time, she earned a master of social work degree from St. Louis University, focusing on health and mental health. She is happy to be the wife of Pastor Kyle Jones. They have three children: Elliott (born April 2015), August (miscarried August 2016), and Owen (stillborn March 2017). She keeps busy chasing after her two-year-old son as well as participating in her church and local moms' group. She enjoys music, board games, and making furniture. Originally from Lee's Summit, Missouri, she now lives with her family in Appleton, Wisconsin.

Reflection 9: Stephanie Traphagan is the wife of the Rev. Bill Traphagan and mother of Sarah and Timothy, as well as Jeremiah Lazarus and Anastasia Leah, who joined the Church Triumphant at eight and four weeks gestation respectively. She can often be found wrangling children in a church pew, reading picture books aloud, and holding two small hands while walking to the post office. Stephanie enjoys baking, curling up with a book and a hot beverage, and solving life's problems with her friends over coffee and a cacophony of children. Occasionally she writes things. She resides with her family in rural Iowa, complete with cows across the road.

REMEMBRANCE SERVICE FOR FAMILY DEVOTION

Light a candle before you begin.

SAY (ADAPTING AND EXPLAINING AS NEEDED TO YOUR OTHER CHILDREN)

The Bible tells us that Jesus Christ is the light of the world (John 8:12): "Again Jesus spoke to them, saying, 'I am the light of the world. Whoever follows Me will not walk in darkness, but will have the light of life.'" We believe that *(name of your child)* has been entrusted to the care of Christ, and we remember the gift God gives us through His Son in uniting us to God through Jesus, and we remember *(name of your child)* by thanking God for His care for *(name of your child)* while *(he/she)* was with us in this life.

READ ALOUD: PSALM 139

PRAY

Gracious heavenly Father, You give life to all living things, and we thank You for the life You gave to us in giving us *(name of your child)*. We entrust *(his/her)* life to You and Your keeping, just as we entrust our lives to You in every moment of every day. Give us peace when we long to be with our child. Grant us Your comfort when consolation seems far from us. Help us to keep Your Word upon our hearts, knowing that just as *(name of your child)* rests from all the toils and hardships of this life, we, too, shall find our rest in You. In Jesus' name we pray. Amen.

SING: "I AM JESUS' LITTLE LAMB" (*LSB* 740)

READINGS, PRAYERS, AND HYMNS
From *Pastoral Care Companion*[10]

SPECIAL SITUATIONS

Because ours is a fallen world, the joy of expectant parents or of new parents is sometimes tempered or shattered by any of a number of challenging circumstances: miscarriage, stillbirth, death shortly after birth, premature birth, medical complications, a decision to give up a child for adoption, or permanent disabilities. Pastoral care at such times concerns not only the child but also the parents and the wide range of agonizing questions, unsettling doubts and discouragement, and roller-coaster emotions with which they may be struggling. As in all evangelical ministry, the comforting Gospel of God's grace and mercy in Christ for us sinners must be the predominating Word.

PSALMODY

Psalm 23
Psalm 77:1–15

ADDITIONAL PSALMODY

Psalm 46:1–5, 11	God is our fortress in time of trouble
Psalm 88	My soul is full of troubles, hear my cry
Psalm 90:1–6, 12–17	Your power overshadows our concerns

---

10   The following devotions and prayers are taken from the books *Pastoral Care Companion* and *Visitation*. The books are used by pastors and deaconesses when making visits. It is possible you were made aware of the books through pastoral or diaconal visits made to you when you lost your child. The contents can be used in the Family Devotional service from Study 3, "How I Will Remember My Child."

Psalm 91:1–4, 14–16	My refuge and my fortress
Psalm 130	I wait for the Lord
Psalm 139:13–18	Fearfully and wonderfully made

READINGS

Exodus 34:5–7a   The Lord is compassionate and gracious

⁵The LORD descended in the cloud and stood with him there, and proclaimed the name of the LORD. ⁶The LORD passed before him and proclaimed, "The LORD, the LORD, a God merciful and gracious, slow to anger, and abounding in steadfast love and faithfulness, ⁷keeping steadfast love for thousands, forgiving iniquity and transgression and sin."

Mark 10:13–16   Let the children come to Me

¹³They were bringing children to [Jesus] that he might touch them, and the disciples rebuked them. ¹⁴But when Jesus saw it, he was indignant and said to them, "Let the children come to me; do not hinder them, for to such belongs the kingdom of God. ¹⁵Truly, I say to you, whoever does not receive the kingdom of God like a child shall not enter it." ¹⁶And he took them in his arms and blessed them, laying his hands on them.

Lamentations 3:22–26   His mercies are new every morning

The steadfast love of the LORD never ceases;
    his mercies never come to an end;
they are new every morning;
    great is your faithfulness.
"The LORD is my portion," says my soul,
    "therefore I will hope in him."
The LORD is good to those who wait for him,
    to the soul who seeks him.
It is good that one should wait quietly
    for the salvation of the LORD.

Romans 11:33–36   God's wisdom is unsearchable

³³Oh, the depth of the riches and wisdom and knowledge of God! How unsearchable are his judgments and how inscrutable his ways!

"For who has known the mind of the Lord,
   or who has been his counselor?"
³⁵"Or who has given a gift to him
      that he might be repaid?"

³⁶For from him and through him and to him are all things. To him be glory forever. Amen.

ADDITIONAL READINGS

1 Sam. 3:18	The Lord does what seems best to Him
Job 1:21–22	The Lord gave, and the Lord has taken away
Is. 43:1–7	Fear not, for I am with you
Rom. 14:7–9	Whether we live or die, we are the Lord's
2 Cor. 1:2–7	God comforts us in all our affliction

PRAYERS

MISCARRIAGE

Almighty God, gracious Father, Your ways are often beyond our understanding. In Your hidden wisdom the hopes of *names of parents* have been turned from joy to sadness. In Your mercy help them to accept Your good and gracious will. Comfort them in their hour of sorrow with Your life-giving Word for the sake of Jesus Christ, Your Son, our Lord, who lives and reigns with You and the Holy Spirit, one God, now and forever. (738)

Lord God, Father of mercies and God of all comfort, we thank You for Your care in this time of trial and sadness. Console and comfort *names of parents* with the assurance of Your tender compassion and unfailing love; through Jesus Christ, our Lord, who lives and reigns with You and the Holy Spirit, one God, now and forever. (739)

STILLBIRTH/DEATH SHORTLY AFTER BIRTH

Almighty and eternal God, You have given, and You have taken away. Comfort *name of parents*, whose hopes have been turned to sorrow. Strengthen their faith in this time of sadness that they may trust in You. Teach them to depend on Your boundless mercy, confident that their little one has been invited into the arms of Your Son, Jesus Christ, our Lord, who lives and reigns with You and the Holy Spirit, one God, now and forever. (740)

Heavenly Father, Your Son bore all our griefs and carried all our sorrows. Strengthen the faith of *name of parents* and all who bear this heavy burden of sorrow and loss. Help them to rely on Your boundless mercy and to trust that their child, who has been gathered into Your loving arms, remains in Your abiding care; through Jesus Christ, our Lord. (273)

PREMATURE BIRTH

Heavenly Father, our lives are in Your care and keeping. Look in mercy upon the fragile life of *name of child/this child*. Preserve *his/her* life, and nurture *him/her* that *he/she* may grow and develop in both body and soul. Grant patience to *names of parents*, and dispel their fears that with confidence they may rely on Your promises; through Jesus Christ, our Lord, who lives and reigns with You and the Holy Spirit, one God, now and forever. (741)

MEDICAL COMPLICATIONS/PERMANENT DISABILITIES

Heavenly Father, we thank You for *name of child*, whom You have entrusted to *name of parents*. Be with this child and those who wait and watch over *him/her* in *his/her* affliction. Grant that Your loving will for *him/her* be done. Encourage the parents with the certainty of Your providential care that they may know Your peace and strength and, relying on You, may bring up *name of child* as one of Your dear children; through Jesus Christ, our Lord, who lives and reigns with You and the Holy Spirit, one God, now and forever. (742)

Hymns

"Entrust Your Days and Burdens"   *LSB* 754:3
"Oh God, Forsake Me Not"   *LSB* 731:4

Additional Hymns

"Great Is Thy Faithfulness"   *LSB* 809
"In the Very Midst of Life"   *LSB* 755:2
"What God Ordains Is Always Good"   *LSB* 760

YOUR CHILD IS WITH THE LORD

From *Visitation*

CHILDBIRTH—FOR STILLBORN, DEATH SHORTLY AFTER BIRTH, OR MISCARRIAGE

> [David] said, "While the child was still alive, I fasted and wept, for I said, 'Who knows whether the LORD will be gracious to me, that the child may live?' But now he is dead. Why should I fast? Can I bring him back again? I shall go to him, but he will not return to me."
>
> 2 Samuel 12:22–23

It seems the most terrible of injustices that a baby, barely knit together in the womb, should die. For those who have lived to 70 or more, we say, "At least she lived to a good old age." Even when young people die, we have memories of the games they played or the work they did. We knew them as individuals. Why does God take the helpless and leave those who are practiced in their sin? Why does He let parents outlive children?

We should know that your baby is not in pain or suffering. We may share David's hope that his uncircumcised newborn infant is with the Lord (2 Samuel 12:23). We, like David, know that God is a God of mercy and loving-kindness. He binds us to Baptism as the means of grace appropriate for bringing faith and forgiveness to infants, but God may have a method that He does not reveal to us whereby He works faith in infants of the faithful who for some reason could not be baptized. Because we do not know, we should not neglect baptizing infants. God's will is always for the best, and we do know that it is the will of our

Savior, Jesus, to receive even infants (Luke 18:15).

Indeed, your baby is not suffering. Could there be anything better for your child than to be knit together according to the Lord's handiwork and then to be received into His eternal kingdom? We on this earth have months or years of toil and hardship yet to endure, and we see Jesus only by faith. We may hope your child sees Him now, face-to-face, that your child is comforted now, even if we are not fully.

Our Lord Jesus Christ does remain with us to comfort us in our sorrow. He was conceived and knit together in Mary's womb, born as an infant to redeem even infants, and suffered on the cross to receive into Himself the suffering of all people. He receives your sorrow now and unites you to Himself—and, we may presume, to your baby—when you gather with all the company of heaven in the worship of the Church and sing, "Holy, Holy, Holy" and eat and drink His body and blood. Our Lord is with you even as He prepares a place for you and promises you, "Let the little children come to Me and do not hinder them, for to such belongs the kingdom of heaven" (Matthew 19:14).

PRAYER

Almighty God, by the death of Your Son Jesus Christ You destroyed death and redeemed and saved Your little ones. By His bodily resurrection You brought life and immortality to light so that all who die in Him abide in peace and hope. Receive our thanks for the victory over death and the grace that He won for us. Keep us in everlasting communion with all who wait for Him on earth and with all in heaven who are with Him, for He is the resurrection and the life, even Jesus Christ, our Lord. Amen. (*LSB Agenda*, p. 139)

THE KINGDOM BELONGS TO CHILDREN, NOW AND FOREVER

From *Visitation*

DEATH OF A CHILD

Jesus said, "Let the little children come to Me and do not hinder them, for to such belongs the kingdom of heaven."

Matthew 19:14

These words are spoken not only now, at the passing of your child, but they were spoken at the birth of your child. That is, they were spoken at your child's new birth by water and the Spirit. As part of the baptismal service, these words remind us that children, though they do not have the maturity of adults, are received by our Lord Jesus. In Baptism, your child received the kingdom of heaven. Jesus' words are a promise to you that even now your child is with Jesus in heaven.

In fact, Jesus' words tell us that not only are children received by Him but children also are those to whom heaven belongs. Just as the weak in Christ are strong and the poor are rich, so also the children are the faithful ones. In this account, Jesus teaches us not to keep children from His presence, from hearing His Word. Even as you brought your child to be baptized, to worship, and even to the altar with you, you brought your child to Jesus. Your child was a faithful one.

Your child now lives with Jesus, yet you remain here in sorrow. But Jesus is also with you here. Even as you long for fellowship with your child, Jesus, who binds us to each other on earth, also binds us to those with Him in heaven. Christians are not separated into those in heaven and those on earth. Rather, all who are baptized into Christ have received forgiveness of sins and are united as the Church, His saints, whether in heaven or on earth. Wherever Jesus is, there are His saints.

Even as Christ rules in heaven, He also lives as your friend here. Jesus takes on your burdens and gives you the blessings of heaven. He mourns with you as you mourn your child, and as you partake of His body and blood, He strengthens your fellowship with Himself and with your child. At the altar of God, you are as close to your child as ever, for your child worships at the heavenly altar even as you worship at the earthly one. Nothing can separate you from this spiritual fellowship with your child. Even if for a little while you cannot hold your child in your arms, you are both held in the arms of your Savior. Your fellowship remains forever in the Lamb.

PRAYER

O Lord, heavenly Father, comfort these parents and their family who grieve the loss of their dear child. Enable them in steadfast faith and confident hope to look for the blessed day of the completion of our salvation, when all who trust in You shall meet again in heavenly joy and glory; through Jesus Christ, our Lord. Amen. (*LSB Agenda*, p. 114)

CHILDBIRTH—FOR STILLBORN, DEATH SHORTLY AFTER BIRTH, OR MISCARRIAGE

O Lord God, Your ways are often hidden, unsearchable, and beyond our understanding. For reasons beyond our knowing You have turned the hopes of these parents from joy to sadness, and now You desire that in humble faith we bow before Your ordering of these events. You are the Lord. You do what You know to be good. In their hour of sorrow, comfort them with Your life-giving Word, for the sake of Jesus Christ, Your Son, our Lord. Amen. (*LW Little Agenda*, pp. 106–7)

"THE COBRA HAS MISSED"

ISAIAH 11:1–9

SERMON FOR THE FUNERAL OF JAMES JOSEPH KELLER BY PASTOR HANS FIENE

APRIL 10, 2017

When God created man, He created him to live forever. And yet, here we are, preparing to bury a child who never lived for a moment outside the womb. When God formed us from the dust of the ground, He built our lungs to breathe eternally, our eyes to see without ceasing. And yet here we are, mourning a child who never drew his first breath and never opened his eyes. God did not create James Joseph Keller to die. So why did he?

"Now the serpent was more crafty than any other beast of the field that the LORD God had made.

"He said to the woman, 'Did God actually say, "You shall not eat of any tree in the garden"?'"

Quickly, Eve fell for Satan's deception. She believed his lie that she needed the fruit that God had forbidden, and in moments, Adam and Eve had disobeyed God, and Satan succeeded in bringing sin and death into the world. Now all men became sinners. Now all men would die. Now sickness and disease, sorrow and hardship would afflict Adam, Eve, and all their offspring. God created His world to be a place of joy. Satan corrupted it and fashioned it into a place of sorrows.

Because of Satan, the wolf now devours the lamb, disease devours our flesh, and sorrow devours our hearts, especially today. Because of Satan, the leopard now preys upon the young goat, and sin preys upon us, filling our hearts with anger and bitterness, unbelief and despair, transgressions we commit in every day of our lives, and transgressions that prove to be especially tempting in an hour of sorrow like this.

Because of Satan, the lion now tears its victims apart, and sin has torn us apart today. So we look out at a world that we've filled with our cruelty and our pride, our lust and greed, our selfishness and self-righteousness, and we feel the pain of guilt, the pain of knowing that we have only brought more fallenness to this world. And at the same time, we look at this little casket, and we are torn apart because James is no longer in this world with us, fallen as it may be.

We are here today because Satan brought sin and death into this world. We are here burying James Joseph Keller because the cobra has burst from his hole and lashed out at this child before he could even begin to nurse.

But the cobra has missed. The serpent has failed. The devil who aimed his venom in the direction of this little boy has instead impaled his fangs in the heel of Jesus Christ.

"There shall come forth a shoot from the stump of Jesse, and a branch from his roots shall bear fruit." So says God through the prophet Isaiah in our Old Testament Reading for today. In other words, when the world was burned over with sin and death, when the mighty tree of God's people was nothing but ashes and a stump, God had mercy on the world, on His people, and promised to restore the perfection of His creation. God brought forth a shoot from that stump. God brought forth His Son, Jesus Christ, born of woman, born to undo the work of the devil, born to rid this world of sin and death, born to crush the serpent's head and restore the perfection of God's creation.

And that's exactly what He has done. So when Satan tried to visit death upon James, he ran right into Jesus Christ, who crushed him beneath the weight of His righteousness. When the devil tried to end the life of this little boy, Jesus struck that serpent dead and clothed James in His forgiveness and salvation, just as He did for you and me. When Satan tried to close the eyes of James forever, the Good Shepherd closed His own eyes at Calvary, crushed the serpent's head, and gave His little lamb the right to look upon His face forever.

Three days later, Satan was still dead, but Jesus lived. Three days after dying to rid the world of sin, Jesus rose to show that those who belonged to Him would live forever in a new creation that would never again be corrupted. Three days after Satan sunk his fangs into the heel of our Lord, Jesus tossed the devil's carcass aside, opened the doors of heaven to His Church, and invited James and all His faithful to live with Him in paradise forever.

So Christ has won the victory. Christ has conquered death. Christ has walked with His resurrected feet to the top of God's holy mountain and restored His creation. There, from that holy mountain, Jesus rules a kingdom where there is no suffering, no sin, no disease, no dying words, or final breath. There Jesus welcomes into this kingdom all who believe. There Jesus pours out His love on all those He claims as His own. There, from the top of that holy mountain, Jesus now holds James in His arms. And on the Last Day, we will see that little boy shining in the glory that God created him to wear forever.

So because of Jesus, the day has come and is coming when the wolf will dwell with the lamb, the day is coming when disease will no longer devour our flesh, and the day is coming when all the sorrow of this morning will be forgotten because we will watch James open his eyes of flesh for the first time, gaze upon the face of his mother and father, his brothers and sister, and gaze upon the face of his Savior. Because of Jesus, the day has come and is coming when the leopard shall lie down with the young goat, the day is coming when sin shall no longer prey upon us, and the day is coming when we will watch Jesus cradle James in His nail-pierced hands without ceasing.

Because of Jesus, the day has come and is coming when the lion shall eat straw like the ox, the day is coming when sin shall no longer tear us apart, and the day is coming when we will watch Jesus feed

James with His righteousness forever.

"The nursing child shall play over the hole of the cobra, and the weaned child shall put his hand on the adder's den. They shall not hurt or destroy in all My holy mountain," Isaiah says. And the reason he says this is because the serpent is dead. So on the day of Christ's return, James Joseph Keller will stand over the hole of the cobra who tried to destroy him, and he will boast of the victory that Jesus has placed into his hands. On the day of the resurrection, James will put his hand into the den of the adder to mock the devil who tried to take his life but only succeeded at placing him into the arms of his God and his Savior.

When God created James, He created him to live forever. And even though we are here today to bury this little child, James will live forever because that's what God the Father created him to do and that's what Jesus Christ, the Son of God, ensured at the cross. When God formed the son of Erich and Susan, He built his lungs to breathe eternally and his eyes to see without ceasing. And because of Christ and His forgiveness, James will forever breathe the air of Christ's righteousness in glory and forever look upon the face of His Lord. God did not create James Joseph Keller to die. And because Jesus died and rose again for James, then James is not dead. He is only sleeping. Cling to Christ and His salvation, and you will be there when he wakes.

COMFORT FOR WOMEN WHO HAVE HAD A MISCARRIAGE

By Dr. Martin Luther, 1542
Translated by James Raun

INTRODUCTION

As preacher in the town church of Wittenberg, professor at the university, and an active church administrator, John Bugenhagen was a close associate of Luther in the Reformation. He served on the committee for Luther's Bible translation, officiated at Luther's wedding, and preached the sermon at Luther's funeral.

In 1541, Bugenhagen had written an interpretation of Psalm 29 and dedicated it to King Christian III of Denmark, where he had introduced the Reformation in 1537. Before sending the manuscript to the printer, Bugenhagen showed it to Luther. Luther's eye caught a reference to "little children" in the text, whereupon he suggested that Bugenhagen ought to add a word of comfort for women whose children had died at birth or had been born dead and could not be baptized. Bugenhagen, however, was not disposed to add such an appendix, though he did not disagree with Luther in principle. He had written what he felt God gave him to say and did not think it proper to go into this subject himself. However, he said he was willing to add any statement Luther might care to make on the subject. Luther agreed to prepare such a statement. Thus this brief but significant piece is an appendix that has outlived the book to which it had originally been attached.

This short item is a significant statement by Luther regarding the fate of children who die before they can be baptized—a borderline theological question of considerable anguish to grieving mothers. It is just such a person that Luther has in mind, not the sophomoric, speculative thinker.

Writing with pastoral concern, Luther points out that the miscarriage (where it is not due to deliberate carelessness) is not a sign of God's anger. God's judgment is and must remain hidden from us. Luther sees the basis for Christian consolation in the unspoken prayers of the mother in which the Spirit is at work and which sanctify the child, and in the prayers of the Christian congregation.

This item appeared in three editions of Bugenhagen's exposition of Psalm 29, published in 1542, in five subsequent editions, and in a Latin edition. It was then incorporated in the various editions of Luther's collected works. This translation is based on the German text, *Ein Trost den Weibern, welchen es ungerade gegangen ist mit Kindergebären*, in WA 53:(202) 205–8.

COMFORT FOR WOMEN WHO HAVE HAD A MISCARRIAGE

A final word[1]—it often happens that devout parents, particularly the wives, have sought consolation from us because they have suffered such agony and heartbreak in childbearing when, despite their best intentions and against their will, there was a premature birth or miscarriage and their child died at birth or was born dead.

One ought not to frighten or sadden such mothers by harsh words because it was not due to their carelessness or neglect that the birth of the child went off badly. One must make a distinction between them and those females who resent being pregnant, deliberately neglect their child, or go so far as to strangle or destroy it. This is how one ought to comfort them.

First, inasmuch as one cannot and ought not know the hidden judgment of God in such a case—why, after every possible care had been taken, God did not allow the child to be born alive and be baptized—these mothers should calm themselves and have faith that

God's will is always better than ours, though it may seem otherwise to us from our human point of view. They should be confident that God is not angry with them or with others who are involved. Rather is this a test to develop patience. We well know that these cases have never been rare since the beginning and that Scripture also cites them as examples, as in Psalm 58 [:8], and St. Paul calls himself an abortivum, a misbirth or one untimely born.[2]

Second, because the mother is a believing Christian it is to be hoped that her heartfelt cry and deep longing to bring her child to be baptized will be accepted by God as an effective prayer. It is true that a Christian in deepest despair does not dare to name, wish, or hope for the help (as it seems to him) which he would wholeheartedly and gladly purchase with his own life were that possible, and in doing so thus find comfort. However, the words of Paul, Romans 8 [:26–27], properly apply here: "Likewise the Spirit helps us in our weakness; for we do not know how to pray as we ought (that is, as was said above, we dare not express our wishes), rather the Spirit himself intercedes for us mightily with sighs too deep for words. And he who searches the heart knows what is the mind of the Spirit," etc. Also Ephesians 3 [:20], "Now to him who by the power at work within us is able to do far more abundantly than all that we ask or think."

One should not despise a Christian person as if he were a Turk, a pagan, or a godless person. He is precious in God's sight and his prayer is powerful and great, for he has been sanctified by Christ's blood and anointed with the Spirit of God. Whatever he sincerely prays for, especially in the unexpressed yearning of his heart, becomes a great, unbearable cry in God's ears. God must listen, as he did to Moses, Exodus 14 [:15], "Why do you cry to me?" even though Moses couldn't whisper, so great was his anxiety and trembling in the terrible troubles that beset him. His sighs and the deep cry of his heart divided the Red Sea and dried it up, led the children of Israel across, and drowned Pharaoh with all his army,[3] etc. This and even more can be accomplished by a true, spiritual longing. Even Moses did not know how or for what he should pray—not knowing how the deliverance would be accomplished—but his cry came from his heart.

Isaiah did the same against King Sennacherib[4] and so did many other kings and prophets who accomplished inconceivable and impossible things by prayer, to their astonishment afterward. But before that they would not have dared to expect or wish so much of God. This means to receive things far higher and greater than we can understand or pray for, as St. Paul says, Ephesians 3 [:20], etc. Again, St. Augustine declared that his mother was praying, sighing, and weeping for him, but did not desire anything more than that he might be converted from the errors of the Manicheans[5] and become a Christian.[6] Thereupon God gave her not only what she desired but, as St. Augustine puts it, her "chiefest desire" (*cardinem desideriieius*), that is, what she longed for with unutterable sighs—that Augustine become not only a Christian but also a teacher above all others in Christendom.[7] Next to the apostles Christendom has none that is his equal.

Who can doubt that those Israelite children who died before they could be circumcised on the eighth day were yet saved by the prayers of their parents in view of the promise that God willed to be their God. God (they say) has not limited his power to the sacraments, but has made a covenant with us through His Word.[8] Therefore we ought to speak differently and in a more consoling way with Christians than with pagans or wicked people (the two are the same), even in such cases where we do not know God's hidden judgment. For he says and is not lying, "All things are possible to him who believes" [Mark 9:23], even though they have not prayed, or expected, or hoped for what they would have wanted to see happen. Enough has been said about this. Therefore one must leave such situations to God and take comfort in the thought that he surely has heard our unspoken yearning and done all things better than we could have asked.

In summary, see to it that above all else you are a true Christian and that you teach a heartfelt yearning and praying to God in true faith, be it in this or any other trouble. Then do not be dismayed or grieved about your child or yourself, and know that your prayer is pleasing to God and that God will do everything much better than you can comprehend or desire. "Call upon me," he says in Psalm 50

[:15], "in the day of trouble; I will deliver you, and you shall glorify me." For this reason one ought not straightway condemn such infants for whom and concerning whom believers and Christians have devoted their longing and yearning and praying. Nor ought one to consider them the same as others for whom no faith, prayer, or yearning are expressed on the part of Christians and believers. God intends that his promise and our prayer or yearning which is grounded in that promise should not be disdained or rejected, but be highly valued and esteemed. I have said it before and preached it often enough: God accomplishes much through the faith and longing of another, even a stranger, even though there is still no personal faith. But this is given through the channel of another's intercession, as in the gospel Christ raised the widow's son at Nain because of the prayers of his mother apart from the faith of the son.[9] And he freed the little daughter of the Canaanite woman from the demon through the faith of the mother apart from the daughter's faith.[10] The same was true of the king's son, John 4 [:46–53], and of the paralytic and many others of whom we need not say anything here.

NOTES

1. Luther wrote this item to be appended to Bugenhagen's exposition of Psalm 29.

2. Cf. 1 Cor. 15:8.

3. Exod. 14:26–28.

4. Cf. Isa. 37:4.

5. As a young man Augustine (354–430) adhered to the philosophy of the Persian teacher Manes (ca. 215–275), which was based on a dualism of light and darkness.

6. *Confessions*, 5, 8; cf. F. J. Sheed (trans.), *The Confessions of St. Augustine* (New York: Sheed and Ward, 1943), p. 931.

7. Augustine subsequently became bishop of Hippo. His thinking has played a significant role in Christian theology and had considerable influence upon Luther, who frequently quoted from his writings.

8. At this point the edition of Luther's works by Enders (vol. XV, pp. 55–56) includes some additional material as cited in WA 53, 207, n. 1: "that he could without the [word and sacrament] and in ways unknown to us save the unbaptized infants as he did for many in the time of the law of Moses (even kings) apart from the law, such as, Job, Naaman, the king of Nineveh, Babylon, Egypt, etc. However, he did not want the law to be openly despised, but upheld under threat of the punishment of an eternal curse.

   "So I consider and hope that the good and merciful God is well-intentioned toward these infants who do not receive baptism through no fault of their own or in disregard of his manifest command of baptism.

   "Yet [I consider] that he does not and did not wish this to be publicly preached or believed because of the iniquity of the world, so that what he had ordained and commanded would not be despised. For we see that he has commanded much because of the iniquity of the world, but does not constrain the godly in the same way.

   "In summary, the Spirit turns everything for those who fear him to the best, but to the obstinate he is obstinate" [Ps. 18:27].

9. Cf. Luke 7:11–17.

10. Cf. Matt. 15:22–28.

EXPLANATION OF THE APOSTLES' CREED

THE FIRST ARTICLE: CREATION

I believe in God, the Father Almighty, Maker of heaven and earth.

What does this mean?

I believe that God has made me and all creatures; that He has given me my body and soul, eyes, ears, and all my members, my reason and all my senses, and still takes care of them.

He also gives me clothing and shoes, food and drink, house and home, wife and children, land, animals, and all I have. He richly and daily provides me with all that I need to support this body and life.

He defends me against all danger and guards and protects me from all evil.

All this He does only out of fatherly, divine goodness and mercy, without any merit or worthiness in me. For all this it is my duty to thank and praise, serve and obey Him.

This is most certainly true.

THE SECOND ARTICLE: REDEMPTION

[I believe] in Jesus Christ, His only Son, our Lord, who was conceived by the Holy Spirit, born of the Virgin Mary, suffered under Pontius Pilate, was crucified, died and was buried. He descended into hell. The third day He rose again from the dead. He ascended into heaven and sits at the right hand of God, the Father Almighty. From thence He will come to judge the living and the dead.

What does this mean?

I believe that Jesus Christ, true God, begotten of the Father from eternity, and also true man, born of the Virgin Mary, is my Lord,

who has redeemed me, a lost and condemned person, purchased and won me from all sins, from death, and from the power of the devil; not with gold or silver, but with His holy, precious blood and with His innocent suffering and death,

that I may be His own and live under Him in His kingdom and serve Him in everlasting righteousness, innocence, and blessedness,

just as He is risen from the dead, lives and reigns to all eternity.

This is most certainly true.

THE THIRD ARTICLE: SANCTIFICATION

I believe in the Holy Spirit, the holy Christian church, the communion of saints, the forgiveness of sins, the resurrection of the body, and the life everlasting. Amen.

What does this mean?

I believe that I cannot by my own reason or strength believe in Jesus Christ, my Lord, or come to Him; but the Holy Spirit has called me by the Gospel, enlightened me with His gifts, sanctified and kept me in the true faith.

In the same way He calls, gathers, enlightens, and sanctifies the whole Christian church on earth, and keeps it with Jesus Christ in the one true faith.

In this Christian church He daily and richly forgives all my sins and the sins of all believers.

On the Last Day He will raise me and all the dead, and give eternal life to me and all believers in Christ.

This is most certainly true.

BIBLIOGRAPHY

Chemnitz, Martin. *Ministry, Word, and Sacraments: An Enchiridion.* Translated by Luther Poellot. St. Louis: Concordia Publishing House, 1981.

Just, A. A., Jr. *Luke 1:1–9:50,* Concordia Commentary. St. Louis: Concordia Publishing House, 1996.

Kleinig, Rev. Dr. John W. "Rituals and the Enactment of the Gospel." *For the Life of the World.* June 1998: 9.

Luther, Martin. *Luther's Works, Vol. 21: The Sermon on The Mount (Sermons) and The Magnificat.* Edited by Jaroslav Pelikan. St. Louis: Concordia Publishing House, 1956.

Luther, Martin. *Luther's Works, Vol. 43: Devotional Writings II.* Edited by Helmut T. Lehmann. Philadelphia: Fortress Press, 1999.

Luther, Martin. WA 53:(202) 205–8: *Trost den Weibern, welchen es ungerade gegangen ist mit Kindergebären.* Translated by James Raun. 1542.

Schultz, Gregory. *The Problem of Suffering: A Father's Hope.* St. Louis: Concordia Publishing House, 2011.

The Commission on Worship of The Lutheran Church—Missouri Synod, *Lutheran Service Book: Pastoral Care Companion.* St. Louis: Concordia Publishing House, 2007.

Visitation: Resources for the Care of Souls. Edited by Arthur A. Just Jr. and Scot A. Kinnaman. St. Louis: Concordia Publishing House, 2008.

BIBLE DISCUSSION GUIDE

CHAPTER 1

1. In verse 54, Paul writes, "When the perishable puts on the imperishable," which indicates that there is a specific time that this happens. When is that time? While this text is specifically talking about the resurrection, it also points to our Baptism, where we put on the imperishable by putting on Christ. We also experience a death and resurrection in our Baptism.

2. How does holding on to the hope of resurrection and victory that we have in our Lord Jesus Christ offer answers to our "why" questions? It may not seem like the answer, but it definitely silences our questions or makes them seem irrelevant this side of eternity. It reminds us of the temporal state of our sufferings and the power Christ has over the grave.

3. What are some of the significant points in Job's confession? Job confesses Christ and His resurrection long before His actual coming. He also confesses his confidence in Christ's victory over the grave in stating, "And after my skin has been thus destroyed, yet in my flesh I shall see God" (19:26). Job's confession is one that is clearly a confession of faith without sight.

4. Why would Christ be a comfort and answer for Job's "why" questions when considering the loss of his children, land, animals, and physical well-being? Job shows what it means to place your heart in Christ as a treasure more than in earthly things. He demonstrates what he believes about Christ: that He does not punish for secret sins or take pleasure in our suffering. Job's comfort comes in knowing that God can make good from that which the devil would hope for evil. He knows that God has a plan for salvation even in the midst of our darkest days, and Christ is that plan. It is in Christ that we also find the hope of a joyful reunion in heaven.

5. At what point in our life, in the whole Bible, and in this passage in particular [Revelation 21:3–5] do we see God "dwelling"

with man? God dwelling with man is Christ Himself, our Immanuel, "God with us."

6. What are the promises in Revelation that our sinful flesh can cling to when facing the death of our children? In verse 4, we are promised no more tears, no more death, no more mourning, no more crying, and no more pain. We are promised that all things will be made new, including our own broken bodies and the broken bodies of our children.

7. In verse 21 [of John 11:1–44], we see Martha making her own confession of who and what she knows Christ to be and to be capable of. Taking into consideration the text from Revelation 21:3–5, what does Martha confess but fail to realize? She fails to realize that in saying Christ is the resurrection and the life, that means His own physical presence was not required to keep Lazarus from dying. All Christ would have had to do was give the word and Lazarus would have been healed or raised, as we have seen with other miracles of Christ.

8. This pericope (specific reading for a day of the Church Year) shows us how death causes confusion and causes us to ask many questions. What is one of the questions asked in our text, and what is significant in Christ's response? In verse 37, the people see Christ being deeply moved and they ask, "Could not He who opened the eyes of the blind man also have kept this man from dying?" Later, right before Christ brings Lazarus back to life, He prays: "Father, I thank You that You have heard Me. I knew that You always hear Me, but I said this on account of the people standing around, that they may believe that You sent Me" (John 11:41–42).

Christ is establishing the source of His powers: God. He is also communicating that the healing He is providing is not just a cool magic trick or something done to appease His own grief at having lost a friend; Christ is establishing that He has power over death. He is as He says in verses 25–26: "I am the resurrection and the life. Whoever believes in Me, though he die, yet shall he live, and everyone who lives and believes in Me shall never die."

9. According to the text, why did Christ allow Lazarus to die? When told Lazarus was sick, Christ responded, "This illness does not lead to death. It is for the glory of God, so that the Son of God may be glorified through it" (v. 4). Later, when it was discovered that Lazarus was dead, Christ responded to His disciples, saying, "Lazarus has died, and for your sake I am glad that I was not there, so that you may believe. But let us go to him" (vv. 14–15). Christ allowed Lazarus to die so that the glory of God might be shown and that people would know and believe that Christ was and is the resurrection and the life.

10. What caused Christ to weep, and why? It is often confused that Christ was crying because His friend had died. While there is truth in this, it is more accurate to say that He was crying for the effects of death upon His friends and the community. The text shows us that Christ cried even before arriving at the tomb. Christ mourned the effects of death upon His friend Lazarus, knowing full well before even arriving that He would raise him from the dead. Christ's tears tell us that He knows how the story ends, but yet He sheds them, knowing the effects of death. He shows us that even with all the answers, we will still grieve and mourn over the effects of death.

CHAPTER 2

1. What was the very first mistake the woman made in this text [Genesis 3:1–11]? She stayed and listened to the serpent and began to doubt the words and instruction given to her. She then continued to converse with the serpent and question what she knew to be true.

2. What caused her to realize that she was naked? Her eyes were open. She knew right from wrong, and as a result she felt shame in her nakedness and guilt knowing she had gone against what God had instructed her to do and had eaten from the tree of the knowledge of good and evil.

3. In Genesis 3:21, the story continues for Adam and Eve, and God does not leave them in shame and nakedness: "And the LORD God made for Adam and for his wife garments of skins and clothed them." What promise of a future plan for salvation does this action hold for Adam and Eve? Can you think of other instances in the Bible where we see the importance of God covering someone's shame?

God covering them with skins is symbolic of the first sacrifice after the fall. This points to how God would ultimately cover all sins of shame, guilt, and fear through the sacrifice of His Son, the Lamb of God.

Several biblical references, including 2 Corinthians 5:2–5, Revelation 3:5, and Revelation 7:9, talk about heavenly clothing that we shall receive from God.

4. Given the brief explanation of the implications of the Jewish law for the woman with a flow of blood for twelve years, how might shame, guilt, and fear have been manifested in her daily life? (Refer to the "Three Ways Shame, Guilt, and Fear Can Manifest Themselves at the Loss of a Child" listed earlier in our study to help answer this question.)

Isolation: She would have been isolated for being considered unclean. She would not have been able to touch anyone without making them unclean as well.

Silence: Hers was a very specific uncleanliness and may have been uncomfortable to talk about in circles of other women, especially since it had been ongoing for twelve years. Even if she had shared, it might have been socially awkward to continue talking about it beyond the general informing of her condition.

Doubt: She may have begun to wonder if her condition was for some unknown sin or if she was even worthy of being healed or of receiving salvation.

5. What actions of the woman with a flow of blood for twelve years might be considered "shameless" acts of faith? She went out publicly; she touched Christ's robe, which made Him unclean according to Jewish law; and she identified herself as the one who touched His robe.

6. How does God coming to us in flesh and blood offer a new understanding for the Jewish community with all their laws for cleanliness and uncleanliness? God, Christ, becomes the new temple, the place to which we go for healing, restoration, and to be made clean. He is the center of community, where outcasts are brought back in, the shamed are exalted, and the broken are made whole.

7. Read Isaiah 53:3–5; then read Romans 5:1–6 and consider:

How does knowing that God knows our shame help eliminate the effects shame can have on our life? Knowing God bore our shame, guilt, and fear helps remind us that we need not be ashamed or feel needless guilt on account of our broken bodies. We can see how even God knows what it means to be enslaved to a body that does not do what it should. God also knows what it means to be naked and exposed before others, and yet He willingly took it upon Himself for our salvation.

8. What is God's answer to the shame we may feel as a result of miscarriage, infant loss, or infertility? For our loss, God gives His own Son, born as an infant into our sinful world. God's answer is His own suffering of shame and His death. Through sufferings, we are brought closer to Christ and His sufferings. On account of Christ, we are given hope through our suffering, which "does not put us to shame" (Romans 5:5).

CHAPTER 3

1. According to this reading [Exodus 12:1–28], what makes a ritual, and what is the difference between a rite and a ritual? A ritual is the overarching concept that includes repeated activities in which groups of people engage. This can include everything from Thanksgiving meals to attending football games. We accept that rituals have repeated patterns and "rules," even if people don't consciously recognize them. A rite is a subset of ritual, and it can be found in the Church. We use the term *rite* in the Church to refer to particular orders of service (e.g., Rite of Holy Baptism, Rite of Confirmation, Rite of Marriage, and Rite of the Sacrament). For these rites, we have specific wordings and rubrics.

Of course, it is accurate to say that "something happens" in the rites of the Church as people receive forgiveness. This is true of the Rite of Baptism, the Rite of Confession, and in multiple ways within the Rite of the Divine Service.

2. Exodus 12 establishes the ritual of Passover. What was the purpose of this first Passover before it became a ritual? First, it served as a sign marking the homes of the children of Israel to be spared by the Angel of the Lord. Second, it served to prepare for their escape from the Egyptians. Third, it created a memorial for how the Lord delivered His people.

3. In the event of a miscarriage, dates are remembered and often filled with some sort of reminder or ritual for the parents. Due dates come and go; delivery dates and birthdays turn into funerals or secularized celebrations of life. But all too often these dates go unnoticed and forgotten by family and friends. What is the significance of the time that Passover was supposed to mark? "This month shall be for you the beginning of months. It shall be the first month of the year for you. Tell all the congregation of Israel that on the tenth day of this month every man shall take a lamb according to their fathers' houses" (Exodus 12:2–3).

The significance of the time in which Passover was held was that it marked a new beginning for them. No longer would they be slaves; God was writing their story, and this was where they were instructed to start; it was to be a part of their lives in the most basic way. There could be no separation of their remembrance of God as His people.

4. Dr. John Kleinig, a theologian, writes that "rituals integrate people with each other in a community so that they can cooperate and share with each other. You can see these most obviously in the function of family meals and the importance of the Lord's Supper in your congregation."[11] With this in mind, what purpose was there in repeating the Passover? The ritual established was to be held as a memorial to remind future generations of God's deliverance and power in the midst of captivity. The ritual served not only as the marking of a people but also as a way of teaching what the Passover was to a generation who had not lived through it. It was a way of communicating a story and returning praise back to God while binding a people in a common story.

5. What is unique about Deuteronomy [16:1–8] and how God instructs His people to go about observing the Passover? God is establishing the Passover as a reminder for the people. Through this

---

11   Kleinig, "Rituals and the Enactment of the Gospel," *For the Life of the World*, 9.

ritual, He communicates His desire to be closely connected to His people and to be the focal point of the ritual. God is the one dictating to the Israelites how to observe the Passover; He is therefore reminding them of how He has provided salvation to them in the past, as well as pointing them to how He will provide salvation in the future (through Christ, His Son).

6. Sometimes it can be tempting to establish rituals that place our children as the focus of what we do and why we do it. How does participating in rituals that hold God at the center help when grieving the loss of a child? (Recall Dr. Kleinig's comment about the purpose of ritual.) When God is removed and something else becomes the focus of a ritual, it becomes meaningless motion without direction. When God is the focus of a ritual, it calls the participant into a more meaningful movement where the direction of the ritual continually draws others in while continually sending praise upward to God. In other words, by making God the center of a ritual, others will be more able to participate and relate, and the ritual can continue for as long as God is being worshiped and others are being drawn in. Our children's stories will only last as long as we remember them, but God's story is one that goes on for generations to the end of time. When we entrust God with the remembrance of our children, He binds His story of life, death, and resurrection to their short lives and creates a more secure and promising remembrance of life than our paltry attempts to immortalize our children.

7. Read Luke 22:7–20. Here we see Christ fulfilling what was promised in Exodus 12 (deliverance not only from earthly oppressive rulers but, more important, from our sins). Why is this fulfillment important today as we grieve the loss of a child? The children of Israel waited for the fulfillment of the promise and the covenant God made with them. They waited and continued practicing the ritual of Passover for generations beyond the very first Passover to keep the story of God's salvation alive among them. Christ's fulfillment of the covenant in becoming the all-atoning sacrificial Lamb changes our involvement in the story. We are brought into the story in the same way the expectant children of Israel were. We now participate not in a ritual of sacrificial payment for our sins, but rather in a rite of reception where we receive Christ's forgiveness and fellowship. Recall 1 Corinthians 10:16–17: "The cup of blessing that we bless, is it not a participation in the blood of Christ? The bread that we break, is it not a participation in the body of Christ? Because there is one bread, we who are many are one body, for we all partake of the one bread."

Having the Rite of Communion is our remembrance of what Christ fulfilled for us on the cross. It draws us in to be partakers in His death and also in the suffering of our brothers and sisters in Christ. We are not alone in suffering miscarriage. Many other women in the faith also suffer the same, and our Savior knows as well what it means to grieve and suffer.

8. Christ, a teacher and the Son of God, would have known all the Psalms. A Jewish boy would have been very familiar with the Psalms as they were read in the synagogue. Why would Christ draw attention to Psalm 22 while He was dying on the cross? (Think on the third point regarding how rituals help in time of grieving.) In referencing just the first few words of Psalm 22, Christ was drawing attention to the whole of Psalm 22, which all good Jewish boys would have known. In reading Psalm 22, it is obvious that it was prophetic and that Christ was fulfilling the prophecies of the Messiah. Part of this fulfillment is seen in Passover, where Christ becomes our Passover Lamb.

9. How does reflecting on Christ and His suffering as a part of ritual become helpful while grieving the loss of a child? Read 2 Corinthians 1:3–6 to help you in your understanding and answer.

> Blessed be the God and Father of our Lord Jesus Christ, the Father of mercies and God of all comfort, who comforts us in all our affliction, so that we may be able to comfort those who are in any affliction, with the comfort with which we ourselves are comforted by God. For as we share abundantly in Christ's sufferings, so through Christ we share abundantly in comfort too. If we are afflicted, it is for your comfort and salvation; and if we are comforted, it is for your comfort, which you experience when

you patiently endure the same sufferings that we suffer.

Grief can consume a person so that he or she is unable to see outside the person's own pain and suffering. Reflecting on Christ and His suffering allows a person to focus on suffering that was willfully endured for his or her own personal benefit. Making time to reflect on Christ and His suffering as a part of ritual allows the answer to a person's tragic question of "Why does God allow me to suffer?" to be present while trying to make sense of his or her grief. Verses 9 and 10 of Psalm 22 offer great comfort when contemplating the loss of a child in the womb. Those who put their faith in Christ cast their child upon God. They remember that Christ did not spare His own life when He came to save us, but He willingly gave it up to make a way to Him. In remembering His suffering and death, our minds are drawn to His promises as opposed to our temporal burdens. While the grief from the loss of a child will never leave us, our burden can be lightened by keeping our focus on Christ and His suffering for us.

10. If we understand a rite to be the marking within a ritual that signifies the changing of a person from one status of being into another—for example, Baptism, confirmation, or marriage—then why would a rite such as Holy Communion become an important practice after having lost a child? As stated at the beginning of the study, "There are times when we feel we have changed so much that we look for new ways to express and commemorate that change." Communion addresses that felt change with a promise. Read 1 Corinthians 15:51–57:

> Behold! I tell you a mystery. We shall not all sleep, but we shall all be changed, in a moment, in the twinkling of an eye, at the last trumpet. For the trumpet will sound, and the dead will be raised imperishable, and we shall be changed. For this perishable body must put on the imperishable, and this mortal body must put on immortality. When the perishable puts on the imperishable, and the mortal puts on immortality, then shall come to pass the saying that is written:

"Death is swallowed up in victory."
"O death, where is your victory?
  O death, where is your sting?"

The sting of death is sin, and the power of sin is the law. But thanks be to God, who gives us the victory through our Lord Jesus Christ.

CHAPTER 4

1. How is Abraham a perfect example of someone who finds identity in God? All that Abraham is comes from God. God specifically called Abraham out of his homeland to be the patriarch of God's people. All that makes Abraham worth mentioning and referencing is due to God's placing of identity upon his life.

2. How does God challenge Abraham in the identity that God laid out for him in asking him to sacrifice his only son? It is as if God is taking back the very thing He has promised Abraham from the beginning. God is challenging the faith of Abraham in asking him to trust that no matter what happens, God can and will still give to Abraham all that He promises to give him. Not only that, but God is asking Abraham to recognize that all that God gives and promises flows from His hand.

3. What are some of the specific things that Abraham says [in Genesis 22:1–19] that display his trust in God throughout the narrative? Abraham says, "Stay here with the donkey; I and the boy will go over there and worship and come again to you" (v. 5). "God will provide for Himself the lamb for a burnt offering, my son" (v. 8).

4. If God is not a God who desires human sacrifice, and He is a God who already knows the hearts and minds of His people, what is the purpose of testing Abraham in this way? God doesn't need our demonstration of faith, but we sometimes need to be challenged to recognize where we have placed our faith. With our small demonstrations of faithfulness, we find God to be even more faithful. God asks for Abraham's only son but stops him and offers His only Son instead.

God doesn't need our faithfulness; rather, He sometimes can use it to show us just how much more faithful He is toward us.

5. **God promised Abraham yet again after testing him that he would be blessed and his offspring would be multiplied. Yet, Abraham had only two sons. Knowing the fulfillment of God's promise to Abraham, what can we conclude about God's calling and God's timing? (Think of what liminal living means.)** We practice liminal living when we recognize that this life is not all there is, and likewise the death of our children is not the end of a story. We hold the hope of salvation right now, even while we suffer losses here on earth. Abraham practiced liminal living by trusting in God's promise as one already fulfilled. When God promises something, we are free to live our life as if that promise were already fulfilled.

6. **How does having a God who identifies Himself with a broken people become a comfort to a mother or father who has lost a child?** In the midst of brokenness, it is difficult to see how what was lost can ever be restored. Knowing that our God is perfectly holy and perfectly whole and willing to impart and share all that He is with us offers a hope of restoration and comfort.

7. **Why do you think John recorded the event of Jesus giving Mary and His "beloved disciple" to be mother and son to each other in the midst of His death and dying? More important, why did He address the replacement of his mother's son from the cross?** Christ giving His mother to His beloved disciple obviously would have been important to John's Gospel on account of the role John played in the event. The son of the widow from Nain (Luke 7:11–15) was delivered back to his mother, but Christ knew He would not deliver Himself back to His mother after His resurrection, so He gave her a new earthly son. The concerns of God's people are also His concerns, and if He had mercy on the widow of Nain, why wouldn't He show the same mercy to His own earthly mother?

8. **Our status as a mother changes when we lose a child, but our identity as mother does not change. How does having Christ as the foundation of our identity solidify our identity as mothers even in the midst of having lost a child?** God is the one who gives and who

takes away. In our loss, we can know that it is God who first gave us the vocation to be a mother or father and that all life is recognized by God. Because the life of our child is recognized by God the Creator, we can be sure that our identity as mother or father is also recognized by Him.

9. Recall the first three words defined earlier: *identity, vocation,* and *status*. Why is it important to distinguish among them when trying to understand what it is you lost and who you are in the context of your loss? Often we can become confused and think that a change of status changes who we fundamentally are. God calls us to be more than our present status in life, and at the same time He offers us so much more for our personal status.

10. Based on the definitions of those words, who defines an individual's identity, vocation, and status? God is the one who defines our identity and our vocation.

11. How is a secularized identity different from an identity based in Christ? A secularized identity holds no foundation or anchor to which an individual can cling. A secularized identity bases itself on status, which is subject to change.

12. How does our Baptism support liminal living for us in the midst of grief, and what hope does liminal living offer you? We are called to recall our Baptism every day until the day it is completed in our death. By recalling our Baptism while living, we remember that our sufferings are temporal, lasting only until that day when God "will wipe away every tear from their eyes, and death shall be no more, neither shall there be mourning, nor crying, nor pain anymore, for the former things have passed away" (Revelation 21:4).

CHAPTER 5

1. A reference is made in Luke 2:19 and repeated in Luke 2:51: Mary "treasured up all these things, pondering them in her heart." The accounts in Luke 3 then switch to Christ's adult life. What are these references pointing to, and what can be concluded from them? Mary is recalling the story of her Son's life as she, His mother, recalls it. It can be concluded that she shared these stories with Luke for him to include and use for the writing of his Gospel.

2. Speculating that Luke gathered his information for the writing of his Gospel after the death and resurrection of Christ, what more might Mary have been pondering and treasuring in her heart as she recalled the birth of her Son and shared it with Luke? Mary might have been contemplating the manner in which her Son died, all the while thinking of the beautiful, precious memories she had of Him. After His death, her treasured memories may have been tainted with flashes and images of His suffering and crucifixion, which Mary would have witnessed. In addition, as the quote from Dr. Just later notes, her pondering included the recollection of the fulfillment of the prophetic texts that she would have known as a Jewish daughter. The fulfillment of these texts was found not only in the life of Christ but in His sufferings and death.

3. Of all the things Mary witnessed and treasured in her heart—the birth, life, death, and resurrection of her Son—it is easy to imagine that witnessing His death could have tainted all her wonderful memories of being His mother, as it says it pierced "her soul with a sword." Why would it become so important that Mary give attention not only to the horrific manor in which her Son died, but also to the details she had treasured up in her heart, such as His birth and childhood? The death of her Son brought salvation to us all, but the manner in which He was born and His life give testimony that He was in fact the Son of God. Mary's memories would serve as validation of the prophecies that she herself may have had a difficult time seeing as being fulfilled through her Son.

4. What similarities and differences do you see between Hannah's story and Mary's story? Both were blessed by God through the opening of the womb, but Hannah's child was conceived by a man and Mary's Child was conceived by the Holy Spirit. Hannah was probably in her early twenties and Mary was most likely much younger than Hannah. Samuel (Hannah's son) was dedicated to the service of the Lord in the temple, and Jesus was the new temple in the flesh. Both women believed the word spoken to them when promised they would conceive a child and give birth to a son. Both women returned praise back to God at the news of their promised children. Hannah had longed for a child and was begging God for a son, whereas Mary was yet a child herself and was given a child without asking. (There are many other subtle differences that can be seen and assumed from the text.)

5. How does Hannah's story become part of Mary's story and vice versa? Having a son meant that a woman had salvation in a sense, and that she would be cared for in her old age. Hannah's prayer for a child wasn't only answered through the birth of Samuel; it was answered through the birth of Christ. Christ is the Child and the Savior that generations had been praying and waiting for. Both women have a part within the story of salvation: Hannah points to the promise through her own story of petitioning and trusting God, and Mary reflects Hannah's faithfulness through her submission and praise and gives birth to the promise.

6. How do the Magnificat and Hannah's Prayer give us an example of what it means to be incorporated into the greater story of salvation? The Bible is filled with stories that make up the greater story of salvation and remind us that our stories aren't so unique or isolated to our own private, personal events. Mary uses the words of Hannah to praise God for bringing her into the story of salvation in the way He did. This shows Mary's humility and faithfulness as she didn't demonstrate a need to create something new and original, but rather, she saw her own sentiments of praise manifested in the same words of Hannah, even though their stories aren't exactly the same. Mary knew that she was participating in a greater story that had been busted wide open for generations past, present, and future.

7. How does having lost a child bring us into the stories of both Mary and Hannah today? We sing the same song of both of these women, and we recall that just like them, we share the same comfort, hope, and salvation in Christ Jesus. Christ is our link, just as He was for Mary and Hannah. Christ is the one entrusted with the lives of our children, and He is the one who binds all our stories together in and through the cross.

CHAPTER 6

1. Ephesians identifies the Church in three different ways. How does this text [Ephesians 2:20–22] identify the Church? What are the specific words used? The Church is identified as an edifice or building. The words "structure," "joined together," "holy temple," "built together," and "dwelling place" are some of the specific words used.

2. What is the Church to be built upon, and what does this mean for the structure itself? The Church is to be built upon Christ. When it is built upon Christ, the structure itself can stand with a sure foundation.

Ephesians 4:11–16:

> And He gave the apostles, the prophets, the evangelists, the shepherds and teachers, to equip the saints for the work of ministry, for building up the body of Christ, until we all attain to the unity of the faith and of the knowledge of the Son of God, to mature manhood, to the measure of the stature of the fullness of Christ, so that we may no longer be children, tossed to and fro by the waves and carried about by every wind of doctrine, by human cunning, by craftiness in deceitful schemes. Rather, speaking the truth in love, we are to grow up in every way into Him who is the head, into Christ, from whom the whole body, joined and held together by every joint with which it is equipped, when each part is working properly, makes the body grow so that it builds itself up in love. (Ephesians 4:11–16)

3. Read Ephesians 4:11–16. To what does this text compare the Church, and what specific words are used? Ephesians 4:11–16 compares the Church to a body. The specific words used are "grow up," "whole body," "joined and held together," "joint," "part," "grow," and "builds itself."

4. How is the Church supposed to grow according to the above text? The Church is supposed to grow with Christ as the Head, growing into Him who holds the Body together.

5. Why do we also need all the Church's members, no matter

how hypocritical, broken, and unhelpful they might seem to us or others? With all members growing into Christ, we find all of the Church's broken members more effective to grow and help others to grow as well. The Church is to exist to help the broken members not just by helping the homeless outside the physical building, but also to manifest the Gospel to those within her walls. Each broken member points to Christ in his or her need or ability to help others with similar needs.

6. How can embracing our broken selves serve us in our healing and our worship to God? Understanding and possibly embracing the fact that we are broken allows us to recognize our need for God as opposed to continually lamenting our broken state.

7. How can we draw other members of the Church into our lives without feeling we need to cover or hide our weakness or brokenness? We can ask other members to pray for us. We can share our stories of grief and our personal struggles with them. We can specifically ask the pastor to pray for us. We can make others aware of the things that are important to us and help them to know how to help.

Ephesians 5:22–27:

> Wives, submit to your own husbands, as to the Lord. For the husband is the head of the wife even as Christ is the head of the church, His body, and is Himself its Savior. Now as the church submits to Christ, so also wives should submit in everything to their husbands.

> Husbands, love your wives, as Christ loved the church and gave Himself up for her, that He might sanctify her, having cleansed her by the washing of water with the word, so that He might present the church to Himself in splendor, without spot or wrinkle or any such thing, that she might be holy and without blemish. (Ephesians 5:22–27)

8. To what does Paul compare the Church in Ephesians 5 [:22–27], and what specific words does he use? Paul compares the Church to a bride. The specific words used are "submits," "love," "gave Himself up," "sanctify," "cleansed," "washing of water with the word," "present," "splendor," "without spot or wrinkle," "holy and without blemish."

9. What lessons are learned in marriage that we sometimes fail to apply with the Church's members as well? *Forgiveness:* It is easier to forgive someone you have to wake up to every morning. Sometimes it is easier to give up on a person or people that you possibly only see once a week as opposed to forgiving them. *Forbearance:* We choose our spouses and know what we are getting into; on particularly difficult days, we can say, "I made the choice to marry him; I have to deal with it." We did not choose the church members, so naturally there will be people we don't like and people we would rather not deal with once a week. *Compassion:* Concern and compassion are easier to share with someone you share a bed with, but church members can be "out of sight, out of mind." Once worship is over, the problems of others are often forgotten with all the happenings of the week. We might even catch ourselves thinking about what we need to do throughout the week while the pastor is still preaching.

10. In each of these texts from Ephesians, how is Christ identified? *Ephesians 2:20:* Cornerstone; *Ephesians 4:15:* Head; *Ephesians 5:23:* Husband.

11. Why is it important for us to recall that Christ is the focal point and most important aspect of the Church? It is important so that we do not become too inwardly focused and forget why the Church exists: for the preaching, teaching, and receiving of the Word and Sacraments.

12. What happens when Christ is not held as the center of worship and church activities? Without Christ, the Church becomes just a club where motivational speaking occurs and social services are offered. Christ is the reason for the Church's existence.

13. In your own words, how does the psalmist identify the Church [in Psalm 84]? Answers will vary.

14. Sometimes in our grief, we forget why we attend worship. We think, *I have nothing to give,* and so we stop going for a time. For what reasons do we go to church? Simply put, to receive forgiveness of sins and to hear the Word. In addition, we go to be built up into the

Body of Christ. We go to have communion with our fellow brothers and sisters in Christ, and we go to celebrate all that God has given us through His Son.

CHAPTER 7

1. Our Lord begged for the pardon of others while being nailed to the cross. What can we learn from Christ's words "Father, forgive them, for they know not what they do" as we prepare our own petitions of forgiveness? We learn to pray like Christ, knowing that sometimes we are called to pray for people who don't realize the extent of their actions and words. We learn from Christ what it means to pray in all humility for the well-being of others, even when their actions may cause us harm.

2. What were the people doing that required forgiveness, and why didn't Christ spell out each sin He was asking the Father to forgive? The people needed forgiveness for words and deeds—for physically causing harm and killing Christ, but also for the evil things they said in mocking Christ and doubting who it was that He claimed to be. Christ's prayer was an "umbrella" prayer. He spoke simple words to cover a multitude of sins and discrepancies. Christ didn't need to spell out each sin because the Father knew the sins for which Christ was asking forgiveness. In addition, it would have been an exaggeration to address each sin.

3. Why is it important for us to ask for forgiveness from the Father on behalf of others even when they don't know of the sins they've committed? Like the soldiers and people at the crucifixion of Christ, people often don't realize they are sinning or causing harm to others, and if they do realize it, then they need prayers all the more. It is important to ask for forgiveness so that God brings not only forgiveness to the incognizant sinner but also healing for the wounded.

4. Why does Christ become an essential part of the equation when talking about forgiving others and living in community with one another? It is only because of Christ's forgiveness that we are forgiven so that we may freely forgive others. When Christ is removed from the equation, we begin to play "tit for tat" and keep tally of each offense our brother or sister commits against us. This becomes exhausting and taxing for an individual.

5. The woman in the story [Luke 7:36–48] is an example of forgiveness primarily for the forgiveness that Christ gave her and also the forgiveness she would have to give on a daily basis to those who knew her and talked about her. In what ways does this text show that she would be expected to forgive and to love as she had been forgiven and loved? In this particular story, Simon the Pharisee called into question the moral status of the sinful woman, even calling her "sinful." The woman would have had to forgive people for their thoughts, for their nasty looks in the streets, and for whispering under their breath about her. She would probably have had to forgive the women who pulled their children close when they saw her coming near, and the men on the street who talked and pointed at her like she was a horse for sale. More immediately, she would have had to forgive Simon for suggesting that she was not worthy of Christ's time and acknowledgment, let alone His forgiveness.

6. How might being given the chance to forgive Simon for his words grant a deeper healing for the sinful woman in the above text? The woman was able to be the one to forgive others when she was in need of forgiveness herself. It allowed her to practice the very response she was in need of and also to practice freeing herself of the unnecessary judgment of others so that she could more freely express and share love.

7. In the midst of grief, it is easy to be consumed with thoughts and feelings that run contrary to the fruit of the spirit (e.g., joy, peace, patience). What is the prayer of Psalm 51? "Restore to me the joy of Your salvation, and uphold me with a willing spirit."

8. Where do we find Psalm 51 within the worship service, and why? Right before Holy Communion. As we prepare to receive the body and blood of our Lord and Savior, shed for the forgiveness of our sins, we also pray that He would prepare us for such reception by creating a clean heart within us. We pray like the sinful woman that there would be room in our heart only for Christ's forgiveness, and that we would be able to go to the altar knowing that our sins and the sins of those who have offended us throughout the week have been and will continue to be forgiven.

CHAPTER 8

1. Read Genesis 3:9–15 in your Bible. In recalling our history, why is it important to include and understand Genesis 3 as our story as well? Genesis 3 reminds us ultimately why we suffer loss, miscarriage, and death this side of eternity, and it also points to the remedy for our pain and suffering (3:15), which is Christ and His own sufferings and death.

2. Whom does the man blame for his falling into temptation, and what is the order and manner of God's response? Man blames God for giving him the woman who gave him the fruit to eat. He portrays himself as a victim of the woman and of God for being given the woman. God does not respond in anger toward the man for blaming Him; rather, He follows the train of blame being passed from the man to the woman and the woman to the serpent.

God starts by cursing the devil and then prophesying how He would ultimately defeat the devil by sending His Son. He then explains the consequences of their actions to the man and woman, and then finally covers their nakedness and sends them out of the garden as an act of mercy.

3. When grieving the loss of a child, why does it become important to place everything upon God, even if it is blame? Blaming God opens the conversation with Him and also still acknowledges Him as God in your life. Taking your problems with God to Him and talking to Him about them is encouraged. Complaining to others about your problems with God is discouraged.

4. In Genesis 3:15, we see the very first proclamation of a Savior, and in Luke 22:42 we see Christ praying to His Father as the offspring of woman who would bruise the head of Satan. How is Genesis 3:15 the answer to Christ's prayer seen in Luke 22:42? What was the will of the Father? The will of the Father was to bring salvation to all of humanity, and in order to do this, His Son had to die. Christ, being true man and true God, knew that the will of the Father was that He would die to pay for our sins and He would strike the head of Satan.

5. Why is Christ's prayer a necessary one, even when He knew what the will of the Father was? Christ's prayer was a proclamation and an example for us today. It was a proclamation of the fulfillment of the Gospel, and it was an example of how faith acts. Faith acts by knowing the grief and sorrow that will come on account of the cross, and trusting in the will of the Father to bring salvation even when the natural will of man is to hide from God.

6. Where and when are Christ's words "not My will, but Yours, be done" made our own? We pray these same words in the Lord's Prayer when we say, "Thy kingdom come, Thy will be done on earth as it is in heaven."

7. What are some of the complaints the psalmist places before God [in Psalm 88]? More specifically, for what particular things does the psalmist blame God? In verses 6–9, the psalmist accuses God of having put him in the "depths of the pit." As a result, the psalmist says, the wrath of God is heavy upon him, and God has caused his companions to shun him. Later, in verses 14–18, the psalmist repeats the same sentiments in reverse order, saying that the Lord has cast his soul away, hidden His face from him, swept over him with His wrath, destroyed him with His assaults, and caused his beloved and his friends to shun him.

8. Out of 150 psalms, Psalm 88 is the only one that does not return praise back to God. What hints does this psalm provide as to why the psalmist does not return praise, and why is this significant for someone who is grieving? Verses 9–13 give an idea as to why the psalmist does not return praise to God. He says in verses 3–5 that he is near death and he considers himself "like one set loose among the dead, like the slain that lie in the grave" (v. 5). Later, in verses 9–13, the psalmist says that the praises of God's steadfast love and faithfulness are not declared from the grave. The psalmist is making the point that the wonders and praise of God are not known in death, but among the living.

This psalm becomes important because it shows the lengths to which a man must go before he will not be able to praise the God of all creation: to death. At times, our lives may not seem worthy of praising God, or rather, we may not perceive God as being worthy of praise. The Psalms prove that until the grave shuts us up, our lives are to be lived in constant praise to God, even when our praise seems less than convincing.

CHAPTER 9

1. Psalm 139 and the First Article with explanation confess God as Creator. What is the significance of believing and confessing God to be Creator over all when we take into consideration having lost a child? Believing and confessing God to be Creator is to believe and confess that He gives and creates children in the womb. He is well aware of all that goes on within a woman's womb, no matter how she thinks she knows best what is going on. To say "I know my own body" in reference to medical situations is a little ironic when confessing God as Creator; the One who knows your body best is the Creator who formed your inward parts. We see this best illustrated in Ecclesiastes 11:5, which says, "As you do not know the way the spirit comes to the bones in the womb of a woman with child, so you do not know the work of God who makes everything." Believing and confessing God as Creator acknowledges that He does not create and throw away His creations like a sloppy novice artist but intentionally creates with purpose. We may not understand the "why" of the process, but confessing God as Creator trusts that He is the one who does understand, and He "fearfully and wonderfully" creates where and when He wills.

2. How might this confession [explanation of the First Article] and Bible verse [Deuteronomy 32:39] go against thoughts among women who share the common experience of having lost a child, but not a common confession? Think of some of the typical platitudes or words of "comfort" used in circles of those who have lost children. Can you identify how this confession and verse from Deuteronomy can be found comforting when compared with the

false hope that we have been clinging to? The confession and verse go against common thoughts in that they paint God as someone who would allow a person's child to die with the same hand that He used to create the child. It acknowledges that we don't get to make sense of God's workings and reasoning behind giving and taking, but that we are to "thank and praise, serve and obey Him."

Perhaps you have heard something like the following platitudes:

"God has a plan for your suffering."

"God never gives us more than we can handle."

"God wanted him [or her] for Himself."

Often in the midst of loss, things are glossed over to make God seem all good in the midst of bad situations. While God is all good, our definition of *good* and the way in which God is truly all good aren't always the same. It is difficult to fathom thanking, praising, serving, and obeying a God who gives and takes away. A God who would kill and wound is a terrible, fearsome God, and when the effects of a broken world play tricks on us, we want to blame or justify God rather than sticking to what we know about God.

There is comfort in knowing that it is God who gives us everything, without any merit or worthiness in us. When we take time to step outside our grief, we realize that what we deserve is death and separation from God. While death might seem more appealing than continuing to suffer the loss of a child, separation from God would be all the more unbearable. In addition, there is comfort in knowing that in the midst of a total loss of control, God remains in control. We may not be able to make sense of the way in which He controls the heavens and the earth, but resting in Him in the good and the bad times brings us to the last bit of Deuteronomy 32:39, which says, "There is none that can deliver out of My hand." There is security in placing all things into the hands that already hold everything.

3. What comfort can these verses [Psalm 22:9–10] offer to parents who weren't able to baptize their child, and how is the understanding of God as Creator who also makes alive and kills a form of Gospel for someone struggling with the same loss? Psalm 22 demonstrates how God knows His creation even before we do. Jeremiah and Isaiah make reference to this notion several times, especially calling attention to the fact that God called them from the womb (Isaiah 44:2, 24; 49:1; Jeremiah 1:5). Where there is life, the Creator plays a significant role in bringing that life into existence. We believe that all creatures belong to God; therefore even a child not fully formed and brought into the world would belong to God. In addition, if it is God who kills, it is also God who obtains authority to give eternal life to whom He wills.

4. In the Second Article of the Apostles' Creed, we confess Christ as Redeemer. If we were to break down the Second Article with its explanation into four parts—He came, He died, He rose, and He will come again—what would be the key points for someone dealing with the loss of a child to apply to their situation when reflecting on each part?

He came: His earthly life means He came into our flesh and the Creator was created. It means He intimately knows His creation and what it means to be in human form. He knew hunger, pain, suffering, sadness, and tears of sorrow. He knows our pain.

He died: His death means that He is also acquainted with the effects of sin upon the body. What is more, He experienced all the effects of sin without having sin Himself, the final trick of sin being death and all its effects.

He rose: His resurrection means that He overcame death. His conquering of sin, death, and the devil is our victory because it means we are purchased from those very things to be His own and live under Him in His kingdom.

He will come again: His coming again means that we wait and trust in the promise that He will come again to restore all things to Himself.

5. In the Third Article of the Creed, we find the sum of all that is hoped for by those whose faith is in Christ: "the resurrection of the body, and the life everlasting. Amen." What significance does this have in light of the loss of a child and the grief that accompanies that loss? It means all that is broken by sin will know restoration. Unformed bodies will know wholeness, hearts once stopped shall pulse again, and feeble bodies will be restored.

6. The texts above [Romans 5:8; John 3:17–18; Mark 16:15–16; Romans 10:17; Galatians 3:2–5; Luke 1:40–42] follow a train of thought that is intended to lead us to make an educated understanding based on biblical texts about an infant who dies without being baptized. Answer the questions below to follow this train of thought.

What does Romans say about *when* Christ died for us? Christ died for us while we were still sinners.

What do John and Mark identify as being that which saves and that which condemns? (Stick to the text and use only the words from the text.) Whoever believes in God is not condemned, John's text says. These texts do not say that the absence of *Baptism* condemns, but that the absence of *faith* in God condemns.

Where does faith come from, based on Romans 10:17? Faith comes from hearing the word of Christ.

Who carries out or sustains our faith as shown in Galatians 3:2–5? The Holy Spirit carries out or sustains faith.

What caused the baby to leap within the womb as seen in Luke 1:40–42? John leaped in Elizabeth's womb when he greeted and heard the faith-producing Word of God, Jesus Himself.

7. What conclusions can be drawn from each of these texts as they relate to infants within the womb? In drawing from all the conclusions made from the texts provided above, Christ died for us while we were *still* sinners, which means He also died for infants, who are also sinners. The Bible does not confirm that the absence of *Baptism* condemns, but rather the absence of *faith* condemns. Because faith comes from hearing the Word of God and is maintained by the Holy Spirit, we find comfort in knowing that faith and salvation do not come by any doing or work of our own. For this very reason, we baptize infants, to make confession of the very nature in which God creates faith: in our helplessness. We know that infants are able to hear the faith-producing Word of God within the womb because of what we see with John the Baptist.

8. Based on this text [Genesis 17:10–14], what would have been especially disconcerting for David in the fact that his son died on

the seventh day? Circumcision was performed on the eighth day. In the Jewish community, circumcision is what brought a boy into the covenant relationship with God. Technically the child of David and Bathsheba (who was never even given a name) was outside the covenant.

9. What does David's response tell us about his understanding of grief and of where his hope was in time of grieving? David places his hope in God's mercy while the child is living and in His goodness after the child has gone. David entrusted his child to the care of the Lord and incorporated God into his grieving by worshiping Him. It is important to know that worshiping God does not always mean that it is done in lightness of heart and with joy.